THEOLOGICAL POVERTY
IN CONTINENTAL
PHILOSOPHY

BLOOMSBURY POLITICAL THEOLOGIES

Edited by Ward Blanton (University of Kent), Arthur Bradley (Lancaster University), Michael Dillon (Lancaster University), and Yvonne Sherwood (University of Kent)

This series explores the past, present, and future of political theology. Taking its cue from the ground-breaking work of such figures as Derrida, Agamben, Badiou, and Žižek, it seeks to provide a forum for new research on the theologico-political nexus including cutting edge monographs, edited collections, and translations of classic works. By privileging creative, interdisciplinary and experimental work that resists easy categorization, this series not only re-asserts the timeliness of political theology in our epoch but seeks to extend political theological reflection into new territory: law, economics, finance, technology, media, film, and art. In *Bloomsbury Political Theologies*, we seek to reinvent the ancient problem of political theology for the 21st century.

International Advisory Board

Agata Bielik-Robson (University of Nottingham)
Howard Caygill (Kingston University)
Simon Critchley (New School of Social Research)
Roberto Esposito (Scuola Normale Superiore)
Elettra Stimilli (Sapienza University of Rome)
Miguel Vatter (University of New South Wales)

Titles in the series:

Massimo Cacciari, *The Withholding Power: An Essay on Political Theology*
Charlie Gere, *Unnatural Theology*
Andrew Gibson, *Modernity and the Political Fix*
Elettra Stimilli, *Debt and Guilt*
Thomas Lynch, *Apocalyptic Political Theology*
Antonio Cerella, *Genealogies of Political Modernity*

THEOLOGICAL POVERTY IN CONTINENTAL PHILOSOPHY

After Christian Theology

COLBY DICKINSON

BLOOMSBURY ACADEMIC
LONDON • NEW YORK • OXFORD • NEW DELHI • SYDNEY

BLOOMSBURY ACADEMIC
Bloomsbury Publishing Plc
50 Bedford Square, London, WC1B 3DP, UK
1385 Broadway, New York, NY 10018, USA
29 Earlsfort Terrace, Dublin 2, Ireland

BLOOMSBURY, BLOOMSBURY ACADEMIC and the Diana logo
are trademarks of Bloomsbury Publishing Plc

First published in Great Britain 2021
This paperback edition published in 2022

Copyright © Colby Dickinson, 2021

Colby Dickinson has asserted his right under the Copyright,
Designs and Patents Act, 1988, to be identified as Author of this work.

For legal purposes the Acknowledgments on pp. ix–x constitute
an extension of this copyright page.

Cover image: Cappella Bardi by Giotto di Bondone, 14th Century,
fresco (© Mondadori Portfolio / Getty Images)

All rights reserved. No part of this publication may be reproduced or
transmitted in any form or by any means, electronic or mechanical, including
photocopying, recording, or any information storage or retrieval system,
without prior permission in writing from the publishers.

Bloomsbury Publishing Plc does not have any control over, or responsibility for,
any third-party websites referred to or in this book. All internet addresses given
in this book were correct at the time of going to press. The author and publisher
regret any inconvenience caused if addresses have changed or sites have ceased
to exist, but can accept no responsibility for any such changes.

A catalogue record for this book is available from the British Library.

Library of Congress Cataloging-in-Publication Data

Names: Dickinson, Colby, author.
Title: Theological poverty in continental philosophy / Colby Dickinson.
Description: London; New York: Bloomsbury Academic, 2021. |
Series: Political theologies | Includes bibliographical references and index. |
Identifiers: LCCN 2020050383 (print) | LCCN 2020050384 (ebook) |
ISBN 9781350177505 (hb) | ISBN 9781350177512 (epdf) |
ISBN 9781350177536 (ebook)
Subjects: LCSH: Philosophical theology. | Christian philosophy. |
Poverty–Religious aspects–Christianity. | Philosophy and religion. |
Continental philosophy.
Classification: LCC BT40.D5155 2021 (print) |
LCC BT40 (ebook) | DDC 230.01–dc23
LC record available at https://lccn.loc.gov/2020050383
LC ebook record available at https://lccn.loc.gov/2020050384

ISBN: HB: 978-1-3501-7750-5
PB: 978-1-3502-3064-4
ePDF: 978-1-3501-7751-2
eBook: 978-1-3501-7753-6

Series: Political Theologies

Typeset by Integra Software Services Pvt. Ltd.

To find out more about our authors and books visit
www.bloomsbury.com and sign up for our newsletters.

To Adam Kotsko

CONTENTS

Acknowledgments ix

Introduction 1
    Outline of the Argument 5

1 Paradox 9

    Theologies of Paradox 9
    The Negativity of Deconstruction 14
    On the Nature of Paradox 17
    An Inverse Theology 20
    The Political Stakes of Paradox 23
    The Kierkegaardian Move 27
    An Alternative Reading 28
    The Political Theological Implications of Paradox 36

2 Negation 39

    Transcendence as the Failure of Immanence 41
    The Assault against Mythology 46
    The Poverty of Theology 49
    Reconceiving of the Secular 52
    The Radicality of the Proposition 55
    The Roots of Reformation 58
    The Role of History 62
    A Possible Experience of Grace 64

3 Grace 67

    The Nihilism of Grace 67
    The Entrance of the Sublime 70
    Accessing the Possibility of Grace 75

　　　　The Restoration of Tradition 79
　　　　The Aesthetic Solution 83
　　　　The Poverty of Grace 91
　　　　Redefining the Ecstasy of Death 94

4　History 97

　　　　Commemorating Foundational Violence 99
　　　　Monumental and Critical Histories 104
　　　　The Critical Idea 111
　　　　The Vulnerability of the Body 113
　　　　The Role of Metaphor 116
　　　　God, Perhaps 121

5　Violence 125

　　　　Revolution and Reform 126
　　　　The Christian Secular 130
　　　　Divine Violence 132
　　　　Revolutionary Violence 138
　　　　An Ontology of Poverty 143
　　　　The Singular Form of Life 146

Conclusion 151

　　　　Re-engaging the Secular 151
　　　　Whither Theology? 156
　　　　The Idiocy of Theology 159

Notes 162
Bibliography 185
Index 193

ACKNOWLEDGMENTS

There are a number of venues where portions of the present volume were presented in early, draft form, including at the always outstanding International Critical Theory Conference held annually at Loyola University's John Felice Rome Center. In May of 2015, I presented some notes on Theodor W. Adorno, aesthetic judgment, and the tensions between law and grace, and I am very grateful to Stefano Giacchetti for organizing the event and for his support in general.

I am very thankful to the Notre Dame Institute for Advanced Study for an invitation to take part in a colloquium devoted to the work of Msgr. Tomáš Halík titled "The Afternoon of Christianity: Church and Theology for a Post-Secular Age" in November 2015. This opportunity and the rich environment surrounding our discussions fostered many reflections, which have managed to find their way into the present book.

A good portion of this book was delivered in the form of two talks in December of 2015 at KU Leuven in Belgium, one at the Centre for Metaphysics, Philosophy of Religion and Philosophy of Culture at the Philosophy Institute there, and the other for the group Theology in a Postmodern Context within the Faculty of Theology and Religious Studies. I am very grateful for their generous invitations to spend some of my sabbatical time there among the many wonderful scholars that comprise both groups. Both pieces were greatly enriched by the discussions that followed, and I am grateful for the academic camaraderie that so clearly permeates the atmosphere in Leuven. Many thanks to Stéphane Symons, Lieven Boeve, and Stephan van Erp for their kind invitations. Substantially revised portions of one of these talks were also presented at the annual meeting of the Catholic Theological Society of America, in San Juan, Puerto

Rico, in June of 2016. I am very thankful to John Thiel, Francis Schüssler-Fiorenza, Jennifer Newsome Martin, and Hille Haker for their helpful and constructive responses to my work there.

I was very glad to have been invited by Hille Haker to present on the topic of violence within ecclesial structures at a colloquium on religion and violence which took place at Loyola University Chicago in April 2016. As always, the friendly and receptive environment of the colloquium was intellectually stimulating to a high degree and inspiring to my work. Thanks too to Sara Lynn Wilhelm Garbers for her wonderful assistance with this event.

Portions of the chapter on history were presented originally at a seminar "Between Eternity and Historicity: Exploring the 'After' of Christianity" with the Centre of Theology, Philosophy and Media Theory at Charles University, Prague, in May 2017. Many thanks to Martin Kočí, František Štěch, and Gábor Ambrus for the invitation to present my work in such a warm and inspirational context.

No book appears as if sprung from a vacuum, and the present work is no exception. There are many people I would like to thank, just some of those involved in the various conversations and projects I have been associated with over the last few years. Those I wish to thank directly for their friendship and insight, among other things, include Stéphane Symons, Willem Styfhals, Stephan van Erp, Lieven Boeve, Christiane Alpers, Dan Minch, Tomáš Halík, Kristien Justaert, Tom Jacobs, Rafał Zawisza, Grant Kaplan, Adam Kotsko, Joeri Schrijvers, Justin Sands, Anné Verhoef, Martin Kočí, Marijn de Jong, Stefano Giacchetti, Gábor Ambrus, Mark Bosco, Hille Haker, Susan Ross, John McCarthy, Bob Di Vito, Aana Vigen, Tom Regan, John Caputo, Peter Fenves, Glauco Barsalini, and Silas Morgan.

Many, many thanks are due to Kathleen McNutt, Marty Tomszak, Wade Casey, and Evan Marsolek who have been more than capable assistants the past few years. Their tireless work ethic on my behalf, in the midst of so much else going on in their lives, has been faultless, and I am very grateful for their keen eyes and organized sensibilities.

Introduction

The long history of theological debate in the West has often involved an oft-repeated "clash" between more traditional or orthodox theologies and those arising from the margins of such discourses—"from below" as it were, insofar as they challenge any presumptive theology conceived with a view point taken as if "from above." Those in the West have accordingly at times been witness to a variety of "insurrectional" theologies, as some recent interlocutors have described these tensions, that share a number of traits in common with other various reformation, radical-political, and even "death of God" theologies. Such theologies, which often claim to be revolutionary for the field as a whole, are of course nothing new to the history of theological speculation. They frequently only repeat already established patterns and challenges to the status quo. What is new, however, is that, rather than seeing such theologies as they have traditionally been perceived—as heretical, antinomian, revolutionary, or even subversive—they are now being understood, not solely as *separate from* or *in opposition to* orthodox theologies, but rather as *part of* the operations of an orthodox theological perspective. In what can only be considered as a complete rethinking of the field, the general dynamics of reform are more or less now perceived to be bound up with those tendencies and desires that exceed the system, but which are also integral to its self-formulation. They are what Mark Lewis Taylor has called the small but ever-present force of "the theological" working within the orthodox formulations of a much more mainstream "guild theology."[1]

If traditional theological claims were often bound up with justifications for sovereign power made legitimate through doctrines crafted to support God's omnipotence and omniscience—the locus of political theology within Western Christendom—then it has always been the task of radical theologies to introduce a new form of political theology as a constant critique of such structures and legitimations. These more or less "heretical" theologies share a number of traits, though they diverge in significant ways as well. What they share in common is an assault on the oppressive injustices that frequently characterize the exercise of sovereign power and its hegemonic institutions and identities. The crisis of authority that has followed the decline of hierarchical and patriarchal systems in a modern context, however, is one that has been most welcomed to such theologies which favor the immanence of a possible divinity in lieu of any transcendence said to undergird various claims to political power said to be employed by necessity. Hence, in a contemporary setting, we can note the prominence of various feminist, postcolonial, and other contextual theologies that point toward an immanent divinity ceaselessly at work in our world. These are likewise the theologies most frequently to come under censure or to be contested as heretical forces working from within a given ecclesial context in order to dismantle its present configurations of power.

The problem with these challenges to orthodoxy, of course, is that too much focus on the undoing of orthodox structures appears to many to lead toward the dissolution of *all* religious structures, institutions, and traditions—the very thing that modernity often discusses under the heading of secularization. If the tendencies moving toward a radical form of immanence as a challenge to transcendent visions of the divine, and as often mobilized through deconstructive forces, become the dominant force in Western theological thought, then what is left of the identity and nature of theology at all? Is there anything one might take as a foundation for theological claims and the communities that construct themselves upon such platforms? Will these radical theologies leave our world's many religious traditions with nothing substantial to found their most basic theological and metaphysical claims?

As many have already noted, it has become increasingly clear that the entire edifice of theological thought, its doctrinal and scriptural supports foremost among them, has come under close critical scrutiny in the modern period, to the point that many have begun to wonder just what future theological speculation might have at all in this world. Though I do not think that theology will be able to ascend once again to the heights of its previous claims for temporal and political power, I do sense that there may be a slight but profound opening for theological considerations in the midst of a secular world that we would do well to note, even though such claims might appear at first glance to have little to do with traditional theological or doctrinal claims. What I am mainly concerned with in this book is trying to ascertain what such marginal, radical theologies contribute to our overall perception of the future of theology and religious orthodoxy, asking and trying to answer such questions as: What is the minimum theological gesture in our world today? Is this gesture enough to support an identity, tradition, or community? But what if the minimum gesture were actually to abdicate the very definition of whatever theology had historically taken itself to be? That is, what if theology were best characterized by a poverty that emptied theology of its identity? What would be left of theology after such a revolutionary (or what some have called a "pure violence") hollowed out the contents and doctrines of theological speculation? Would this be the only theology left to humanity? And what sort of gift would this be?

Attempting to answer these questions is doubly difficult, however, since, as I have already noted, the radical theological forces that deconstruct orthodox positions are ones that are active from *within* orthodoxy itself. They are not separable from the structures, institutions, and traditions that pass along the deposit of faith from generation to generation. They are rather *necessary* for such processes of transmission to take place at all. Nevertheless, in our current situation, the rise of secularization begs the question of whether or not religious institutions in particular will be able to weather the storm which these deconstructive forces unleash upon the various theological and doctrinal claims that have sustained religion in the West thus far.

It is for this reason that the present study is of the inherent kenotic existence of theology, its own unique *poverty*, as a possible way of opening theology toward secular, interreligious, and comparative exercises, though in such a way as to neither defend nor excessively rely upon the Christian theological domain. Hence, the study relies upon recent continental philosophical interventions in theological matters in order to demonstrate the relevance of a kenotic theology that the field of theology proper has yet to fully embrace. If the poverty of theology is to become the primary manner through which theology demonstrates its relevance to our contemporary secular world, then it is only through its willingness to weaken its own identity that we might, paradoxically, perceive its greatest strength—something that was actually part of the initial theological deposit all along.

More specifically, this book addresses a number of critical forays into subjects that refocus our understanding of the nature of political theology, including theological (mis)uses of paradox in the context of dialectical methods, the act of negation as the greatest sublime gesture within the realm of aesthetics, the possibility of grace in our world despite its apparent absence, how a sublime presence rewrites our relationship to history, and the potential for revolutionary and divine (non)violence as a path toward redefining the future of theological inquiry. Essentially, my argument concerning the kenosis of theology takes shape as each controversial topic in the history of theological thought—violence, paradox, negation, and grace as an entrance of the sublime—is revealed not as forces to be removed from ecclesial structures, but as internal calls for, and mechanisms of, unending reform itself. Taking up each of these subjects in turn before taking a concluding look at their implications for theological thinking on the whole, the final two chapters present a detailed look at the possibility of the poverty of theology as an historical and eschatological horizon that invokes a perpetual series of reforms (as "revolutions within a revolution") toward an ecclesial form that is never historically present, but always sought after. This book therefore merges a number of continental philosophical perspectives in order to illuminate the ultimately unresolvable tension between so-called heterodox and orthodox theologies—another highly significant way of imagining the operations of a theo-politics in a contemporary context.

Outline of the Argument

To gain a better sense of the detailed arguments I am presenting, an overview of each chapter will be helpful. In the first chapter, I consider the role of paradox or contradiction in the Jewish and Christian traditions. First, I follow the work of Tomáš Halík who presents us with a theological call for the acceptance of paradox that is bound up with a rejection of the modern dualism between subject and object. Halík's recommendation for the creation of a space for paradox embraces a "plurality of perspectives" that becomes ever wider in our contemporary period, a perspective that is essential for current and future theological work. In this chapter, paradox is put in conversation with mystical or negative theology as well as Pauline theology and a host of contemporary continental philosophers in order to suggest that paradox can be conceived of as a distinctive logic of dispossession, or of not owning one's own (theological) identity.

Following the claim of critical theorist Theodor Adorno that theology must be entirely transformed if it is to continue to be meaningful, in the second chapter I briefly connect Adorno's negative dialectical method, and so the role of the negative within theological thought on the whole, with

Maurice Blondel's "method of immanence" in order to argue that both authors maintain a solid critique of Kantian transcendentalism and of traditional (Hegelian) dialectical forms while yet creating new forms of non-identitarian dialectics, including complete reformulations of both the "supernatural" and the "metaphysical." This preliminary analysis allows me, throughout the chapter, to rethink the role of the secular alongside figures as diverse as Julia Kristeva, Charles Taylor, Ivan Illich, Giorgio Agamben, and John Caputo in order to see secularization as a force of reform within an otherwise political-theological history.

The third chapter on the subject of grace primarily examines the (theological) aesthetics of Adorno insofar as he frames his work in light of his development (and implicit) critique of Kantian aesthetics. I argue that Adorno points us toward the manner through which the theoretical and deeply historical-theological tension between law and grace (or *justice* and *mercy*) is considered in the sphere of aesthetic formulations, taking shape most determinately through the Kantian definition of judgment. Utilizing Eli Friedlander's recent interpretation of Kant's construal of the dichotomy between nature and art as one that ultimately illuminates the act of "being given" (precisely as an experience of grace), we consider how such a "lawless law" or "formless form" might be a parallel formulation to theological efforts to define a grace beyond the boundaries of law (or rule). The aim of this chapter is to develop an approach to theological methodology that would envision theological aesthetics as more than a reflection on beauty and goodness, but rather as *the* major theoretical-philosophical division at the heart of the Christian tradition, one that shapes our language regarding grace, judgment, redemption, and the (anthropological and moral) boundaries between the natural and the artificial.

The guiding questions of the fourth chapter on the role of history in each of the preceding topics are most directly: How are we to deal with tradition and its myriad ways of molding people? How can one both affirm the necessity of tradition for human life and language while also critically examining it as a potentially deceptive and destructive phenomenon? Following the work of René Girard, I address these questions by reflecting on the role of memory and memorialization that undergird every tradition and the people formed by those traditions. In doing so, this chapter connects the process of tradition with the sublime encounter that certain traditions foster through the creation and maintenance of (religious or pseudo-religious) sites of memorialization. After laying this groundwork, I suggest that a poverty of theology can create the necessary space for the roles of unbelief and the secular within the political formulations of Christianity. That is, perhaps there can be a sublime encounter with the potentially divine O/other who undoes our "sacred" identities and thereby illustrates our vulnerable, precarious selves as a moment of what appears as a purely immanent grace.

The final chapter analyzes the ambiguity of violence as it is utilized politically in order to either prevent self-reflexive structural reform or champion utopian revolutionary hopes when a particular reform agenda appears to be connected to a "violent" system of oppression. By doing this, the fifth chapter takes up the considerations of Hannah Arendt, Walter Benjamin, Jacques Derrida, Slavoj Žižek, and Giorgio Agamben in order to discern just how a critical, self-reflexive awareness within ecclesial structures might be concretely obtainable. As this chapter demonstrates, essential to this work would be a destituent power that renders laws inoperative, not from outside the domain of law, but from *within* it.

1

Paradox

Those who find their life will lose it, and those who lose their life for my sake will find it.

—MATTHEW 10:39

Theologies of Paradox

Among many other places within the Gospels, we hear such a saying, one that is as much enigmatic as it is paradoxical. By suggesting that one give up that which is supposedly most precious to them, their very life, in order to gain life anew, the Gospels frequently portray a faith that has for centuries appeared to many as a paradox, or that which contradicts the coordinates of reason but which appears also as a central tenet of faith. Alongside the Incarnation, the Trinity, and the Resurrection, this recipe for finding true life within paradox resists any explicit definition and asks those who would believe to accept such doctrinal propositions through a faith that appears to contradict the operations of reason. The fact that such articles of faith rest upon a paradoxical structure is nothing new to the history of religion. Indeed most religions dabble often in such formulations that frequently invoke the supernatural to try to resolve the tension or at least placate one's logic.

What has become more interesting to modern commentators on the nature of paradox for people of faith, however, is the manner in which the structure of paradox itself has revealed a deep undercurrent of political implications. In other words, asking people to embrace a paradoxical proposition is likewise a highly beneficial way to secure one's institutional loyalties. Paradox lies at the heart of every community's justification for its own existence, as there is no theoretical legitimation possible for a particular communal identity, the authority vested in the community, and the significance which its traditions accrue over time. There are deep political consequences for utilizing paradoxical positions within a religious communal context, and these need to be better understood so that we might establish a critical political theology capable of redefining the role of the theological within our world.

More recently, and hoping to move beyond such an ideological reliance, the Catholic priest and philosopher Tomáš Halík has taken up in his work a veritable pantheon of authors said to represent a variety of historical "theologies of paradox," including such figures as Saint Paul, but also Augustine, Meister Eckhart, John of the Cross, Søren Kierkegaard, John Caputo, and Jean-Luc Marion.[1] Halík presents us with a theological call for the acceptance of paradox that is bound up with a rejection of the modern and highly rationalistic dualism between subject and object alongside an embrace of the "plurality of perspectives" that only becomes ever wider in this day and age.[2] Though I think that these outcomes are certainly central to whatever future theology is to have in our world, my main concern with Halík's efforts, among others, is with the at times "misty" usage of paradox, its potential linkage to mystical, "negative" theologies, and the political implications that such beliefs hold.[3] As we might recall from certain critiques of the philosopher Jacques Derrida, who repeatedly insisted that his philosophy was decidedly *not* a negative theology, paradoxical thinkers and mystics may ultimately provide, through their very recourse to paradox, another entrance for the assertion of (strong) political identities in other forms—something that Halík himself achieves, albeit indirectly at times, in his own work. The writings of Pseudo-Dionysius, one of the theologians of paradox Halík names, as but one prominent example of such a trend, have been used for centuries to justify a very this-worldly ecclesial hierarchy based on an other-worldly "celestial hierarchy" set by God above.[4] Divine legitimations of earthly political powers were casually brought into existence through recourse to such analogies.

Contemporary accounts of paradox are, for this reason, complicated by a lengthy and highly debated theological history, as well as their proximity to any politics, disclosed or hidden within them. Looking for such an example of the use of paradox that reinserts strong claims of knowledge (and identity) in alternative ways, we might note Jean-Luc Marion's "praise" of (Kierkegaardian) paradox as a means by which to reintroduce identity insofar as paradox can serve as a framework that limits thought from reaching beyond itself, putting paradox into terms comprehensible for determining a "negative certitude" *in* knowledge. This is precisely where specific political stakes are capable of entering the debate, though Marion, at least in this context, does not acknowledge this possibility. In his words, "The paradox does not prohibit the knowledge of phenomena, but on the contrary defines the figure that phenomena must take in order to manifest themselves, when they contradict the conditions that finitude cannot not impose upon them. A way of thinking is measured precisely according to the paradoxes that it endures, and that it calls for."[5] Just such a way of thinking, however, is what Theodor Adorno had once called a "concept fetishism,"[6] or an attempt to "hypostasize irresolvability as a solution to the problem," which he believed Edmund Husserl had done in his attempt to establish a phenomenological epistemology that Adorno was himself set "against."[7] Marion's thought, it could therefore be argued, does not open itself up to a genuine experience of the sublime, but only of overly saturated beautiful phenomenon—a crucial, but perhaps somewhat misleading, step in that it does not contain an account of the political in any respect.[8] Failing to give such an account leaves theological speculations such as these adrift in abstract speculation and, potentially worse, offers dominant political theologies a chance to covertly direct the paradoxical beliefs of the faithful in ideologically opportune ways.

To know the work of Tomáš Halík, however, is to know someone who is manifestly critical of traditional theological claims that would oppress others or espouse a particular political ideology concealed underneath a theological proposition. As a Czech theologian and someone sensitive to the years of Communist oppression that took place in his native country, Halík would certainly not rest content knowing that his embrace of paradox might conceal an active political element that may be oppressive in its assertion of a knowledge that could be used to manipulate those who would believe in it. And yet, there is always the question of whether or not a reading of secular culture as inherently also part of the Christian legacy is not a back door attempt to reinscribe theological notions of sovereignty back into one's worldview, much as Karl Rahner's notion of the "anonymous Christian" can be said to perform a similar act. Therefore, my question, one that will soon expand toward examining the nature of political theology itself on the whole, is this: To what degree might Halík's challenge to systems and structures—something he clearly champions—be bound up with those notions of paradox that are utilized in order to legitimate institutional structures? What difference too might this make in his or other usages of paradox? If the political theorist Carl Schmitt once established his conceptualization of sovereignty based upon the exception as a form of paradox—which I will look at more closely in what follows—what other ways to think paradox might be possible beyond this?

I might first wager that Halík's ultimate position might be somewhat similar to the crypto-theologian John Caputo's, which searches the notion of paradox locatable in Søren Kierkegaard's work looking for another way to understand it in light of his own declarations for a politically "weak thought." Caputo's reading of Kierkegaard, and so the latter's highly influential notion of paradox as well, is that Kierkegaard goes too far in assuming that the temporal cannot in any way house the eternal—"the dialectic collapses," as Caputo puts it—so that Kierkegaard's notion of paradox has the potential to be, in the end, a justification for divine sovereignty that mirrors human sovereign power and so legitimates a sacrificial economy.[9] In other words, rather than the experience of the eternal being that which divides or explodes the temporal from within, the eternal stands at an infinite distance from the finite. This is the distance that is simply accepted as a paradox but which also mirrors the distance that the sovereign has historically maintained vis-à-vis his subjects. In this sense, using paradox as a justification for a governing system or a given economy can become a reinscription back into the sovereign economy from which one was initially wanting to escape. Such a tactic, as we will see soon, undoubtedly avoids embracing Adorno's negative dialectical movement which was an effort to go back into dialectics in order to negate the dialectic itself. Adorno's particular caution with regard to this use of paradox, then, is one that puts a firm contrast between paradox and other forms of (negative) dialectical thought, leaving us to ask the question: "paradox or dialectic?"—the subtitle to a debate between the materialist philosopher Slavoj Žižek, who opts for the latter, and the radically orthodox theologian John Milbank, who tries to rehabilitate the former.[10] This is a debate illustrative of the tension I am trying to illuminate that I will take up later in this chapter.

In an attempt to develop a "negative eschatology" that, I would suggest, somewhat parallels Adorno's negative dialectic, Halík conceives of not only how negative theology might be used to negate any fixed identity of God but also how the one who utilizes negative theology must then, in a further step, not simply reinstate a new identity (*the* typical political ploy of paradoxical thought), but rather remain open to an "inconceivable absolute future."[11] My reading of this second movement is that Halík opens the pathway toward a "negation of negation" that characterizes the permeability of nonidentity (which I will take up directly in the chapter that follows), even if he at times also shares with the notion of paradox as a negative theological exercise that eventually gives way to stronger forms of (Christian) identity. In making this step, he joins with others who have recently sought to develop forms of "ontological poverty" as a "metaphor of openness towards God's gifts."[12] Most significantly, for my purposes here, it is this possibility of a second negation that he hints toward but does not fully develop that also provides us with a possibility for political critique that cannot be overlooked and which turns any theology of paradox away from becoming a purely ideological platform.

The Negativity of Deconstruction

What we have seen so far is demonstrative of recent articulations of paradox within certain philosophical registers that are attentive to the dimensions of the religious and the theological. It might be helpful at this point to note as well the problematics and difficulties of engaging in a negative theology without simultaneously taking stock of its political implications. For far too long, in fact, negative (*apophatic*) theologies have been seen to point directly back at positive (*kataphatic*) theological propositions without taking account of the proper role of negativity within political theological discourse. Specifically, isolating the priorities of a negative force that does not merely seek to (re)turn into a positive, political construct is the task of the present work, as much as it was operative in the deconstructive philosophy of Jacques Derrida. Derrida was someone who "rightly passed for an atheist" but who also claimed to be the last of the Jews, or at least a Marrano figure, one whose identity was split at its root and so internally divided. To be mistaken as an atheist, he would note, was one of the fundamental possibilities for anyone engaged in negative theology.[13] For Derrida, whose deconstructive methods were on occasion taken to be a wholly apophatic exercise, negative theology was focused on a supposedly existent, transcendent being; and negative theology developed itself as an institution with a history and archives of its own, whereas his version of an entirely negative deconstruction was more properly a (negative) discourse on *différance*—that is, on the structural oscillations of language and of the difficulty of (re)presenting anything at all.[14] His insistence on the depiction of a spectral messianic force (along with the eschatological, apocalyptic tone of it) that resisted ever becoming a historical, concrete messianism provided him with a permanent, inbuilt critique of any given representation or structure. This was to be the trade in deconstruction from which, again and again, Derrida would profit, and from which Caputo's and Halík's theologies descend directly.

Like the operations of a truly negative theology, however, Derrida relished the hyperbolic desire characteristic of the paradoxical depths of apophasis to "go beyond" what he saw before him, to "go where one cannot go," such as toward the "possible impossible" or the "impossible possible" for which he often clamored.[15] In many ways, as I will eventually indicate, his search was one for a possible grace that could only be defined as what exceeded the system, *any* system, structure, institution, law, or definition. This is precisely the sense too lurking behind Elliot Wolfson's "hypernomianism," to locate the phrase more precisely, and it runs parallel to how Derrida, in his essay "Envoi," seeks to isolate the "envoi" (or "sending") as an act outside the given folds of representation and as yet explicitly wedded to them, hence recalling as well his work on the aporia that is neither an antinomy nor part of any dialectics.[16]

To engage in a negative theological discourse was, for Derrida, like the act of deconstruction, a hyperbolic exceeding of the limits of language, of "passing to the limit, then crossing a frontier, including that of a community, thus of a sociopolitical, institutional, ecclesial reason or raison d'être."[17] Dissembling the foundations of reason itself, and so of any possible grounds for our understanding, certainly resembles negative theological procedures, which, for their part, were often wholly concerned with undoing the foundations of rationality. The most that one could ever (re)present when speaking of

God, Derrida seems to suggest, would be a form of testimony or confession, not of metaphysical speculation, but rather the impossible possibility of communicating a nonknowledge, of what arrives *after* knowledge.[18] Such a discourse, which really never becomes a discourse per se, was really a *post-scriptum*, that which comes after the writing of the text and which is really more akin to recording a memory than to speculative thought.[19] It is neither philosophy nor theology, neither sermon nor hymn, he will say, for such things are rather texts from which one could not escape.[20] Each maintains a tradition and a canon of writings that limit possibility.

In ontological terms, such suggestions are to speak of nothing, of "less than nothing," of a becoming-nothing that is also part of the process of becoming-self or becoming-God—a phrase that, as we will see, places him proximate to Slavoj Žižek's parallel formulation on the possibility of being "less than nothing."[21] It is, he will say, a "*kenosis* of discourse" that is only capable of offering critique insofar as it impoverishes discourse, and is also always itself "in poverty."[22] What arises from this "*kenosis* of discourse" is no doubt a "crisis" brought on by apophasis, one that destabilizes all phenomenological, ontological, and transcendental discourses.[23] Historically, such a crisis has mainly resulted in theology's attempt to be "something" rather than enter into a form of becoming-theology as a task of becoming-nothing, and so to remain the "queen of the sciences" rather than take a serious and lasting vow of intellectual poverty.[24] But what if, he muses, God were "[…] the name of this bottomless collapse, of this endless desertification of language"?[25] What if the divine were what was to appear as its absence alongside the destruction of our structures of meaning?

As Derrida well knew, negative theology remains active within every attempt to institutionalize theology, haunting and displacing its positive efforts, suspending its every belief, though also, in the end, allowing whatever positive constructs to remain intact, if nonetheless redefined. This situation allows us to grasp something of negative theology's potentially antinomian flavor—that is, its ability to *appear* to be opposed to all legal or normative measures.[26] No institution or tradition is free of its lingering negative theologies, and this is what will cement the overlap between deconstruction and negative theology in a substantial sense. In this play of *différance* there is a great deal of pleasure, opening "a passion to the enjoyment *of* God," as Derrida will describe things.[27] To suggest as much is, of course, a paradoxical way of thinking: that one might find enjoyment in being within the desert of language, of being lost in order to regain one's enjoyment found in the act of play itself. It is a paradoxical way of existing that, to be clear, goes beyond our understanding, but does not leave us devoid of passion. It is, for this reason also, a fundamentally negative exercise within any given structure or institution, and so it is not merely the paradoxical foundation of yet another institution. There is a "negative eschatology" operative in Derrida's work as much as in Halík's, one that forces us likewise to reread the role of paradox in political-theological terms.

On the Nature of Paradox

There are at least two ways to conceive of paradox. On the one hand, that it is the result of possessing something that we should not possess, but then nevertheless seek to justify possessing it to ourselves. On the other hand, that in renouncing our right to possession, we yet end up possessing something but in an entirely different way, "as if" we did not possess it at all. Derrida certainly opted for the latter option, and the difference between the two is crucial for political as well as theological reasons. My initial consideration of this split is that it is only the latter option that embodies the paradoxes that sustain the Christian (Pauline) (non)identity, which, if we are to follow this logic to its conclusive end, is really a logic of dispossession and of not owning (or identifying with) that which we had thought was rightfully ours, in this case one's identity.[28]

The paradox that results from possessing something we should not actually possess, to my mind, becomes politically theologically even more salient in examples wherein identities are held firm and much is predicated upon one's refusal to yield them up. We might take in this regard, for instance, the paradox that insists that the unfortunate definition of loving one's neighbor means at times that you might have to kill them—a paradox that a good many Christian soldiers have felt the need to uphold in some measure throughout history. Such a paradoxical logic is framed by a continuous securing of identity, for it assumes, of course, that one can identify and remain certain of (certain enough to kill at least) the identity of the enemy whom one wishes to kill. That is, the identification of the enemy, or of the ally (or friend)—*the* fundamental distinction for political thought according to Carl Schmitt—will not be undermined from within, revealing a reversal of fortune wherein the enemy becomes capable of being one's friend, and wherein one's friend may turn out to be one's enemy as well.[29] For those "culture warriors" who staunchly defend some semblance of Christian identity in the face of other religious traditions or an ever-expanding secularism, the same understanding would apply, for the fear that their identity will be eroded in the face of vague looming attacks (typically in the West from the encroaching and ambiguous figure of the "Muslim" or the "Jew") leads to the formulation of a paradoxical deity that can in some sense be possessed and so defended.

Referring to the second sense of the term, and here following the analysis offered in the philosopher Giorgio Agamben's reading of Pauline thought, the paradox that results from the realization that we do not possess what we thought we had possessed, that which we identify with or had utilized as the source of our identities, can be derived instead from a Pauline logic that realizes how even the enemy (in the *flesh*) may turn out in the end to be a friend (in the *spirit*) and so in defiance of whatever cultural, political, or religious representation has been placed upon them. In this fashion, we can take note of how the reductionistic representation that is placed upon the individual, and so serves as a negation of one's fuller humanity, is itself reduced (or negated) so that it cannot be the last word used to exhaustively identify the person who truly exceeds whatever labels might be foisted upon them.

When Paul conjectures that he has become "all things to all people" (1 Corinthians 9:22) and so is able to transgress the cultural boundaries that typically define and order society, we are led toward a dispossession of identity that has yet to fully realize itself either within or outside of its theological context. Lest we forget what Paul was really up to, however, we must also note how he was not looking to develop a liminal identity between atheism and the followers of Christ: he was in quest of the atheism that resulted *from* the death *of* God *in* Christ—a major difference in comprehending the point of access to such an "atheism." Indeed, can we even call such an atheism by the same name that we might identify someone as an atheist today? Most likely not, but also most likely a little bit. This is a proposition that should take on a deeper resonance when we recall that Derrida's answer to whether or not he engaged in negative theology was "yes and no."[30]

As Paul Ricoeur once put it, translation is the impossible but necessary task, and, I would add, one that makes our terminological dependencies more than a bit problematic at times.[31] In other words, humanity's dependence upon a particular definition (as identity) is often undone by the act of translation that necessarily accompanies every encounter between persons or communities, even if they employ the same language. This is a paradox embedded within the existence of language itself, and it is one that humans frequently ignore in order to posit what appears as a monolithic linguistic-cultural community. But it is also this paradox that signals something like the possibility of going beyond the imposed representations that some negative theologies actually help to maintain in order to achieve a second negation that reconceives of the possibility for theological operations altogether.

An Inverse Theology

It seems more than appropriate that Adorno's critique of paradox was of apiece with the entirety of his inverse theology, for, as he suggested in his *Negative Dialectics*: "The theological conception of the paradox, that last, starved-out bastion, is past rescuing—a fact ratified by the course of the world in which the *skandalon* that caught Kierkegaard's eye is translated into outright blasphemy."[32] Adorno's dismissal of theology's last remaining metaphysical concept, the paradox, is brief: it appears to be a decaying form of dialectics, a dialectics which, he would aim to illustrate, should rather be gone into further and negated, rather than made co-conspirator in an attempt to go beyond dialectics but only thereby extend its reach that much further toward a fading horizon. The demise of paradox as being able to grant one's metaphysical speculation a theological imprimatur seems to be legitimated in his eyes by the fact that the *skandalon* that should have originally motivated theological discourse to give a defense of how it is not actually a scandal to the world is not perceived for what it is—it is "translated into outright blasphemy" rather than utilized as the underlying fuel of its discourse.

Adorno's insight should be nothing new to theological conversation, for the scandal that was Christ was the scandal that should not have been found in Christ, for he was only a scandal to those who misperceived his message: blessed is the one who sees that Jesus is not the *skandalon* (Matthew 11:6; Luke 7:23)—another paradoxical statement. Scandal, in the terminology of cultural theorist René Girard, is fueled as well by the "feverish desire to differentiate between the guilty and the innocent": it is the bedrock of sacrificial violence and it is that which Jesus rejected as tied in any way with his project of exposing such scapegoating mechanisms.[33] Scandal involves those persons whose identity cannot be determined, the hybrid identities of boundary-crossers who seemingly maintain the space of nonidentity and who are most likely to be scapegoated, or excluded from the community, but who also have a unique sense of what the failure of identity feels like in concrete political-theological terms.

Adorno's point is therefore well-taken that the scandal that Jesus embodied was not recognized for what it was, what we might now, following Girard, truly call an anti-*skandalon*. Might there then be another way to recover the concept of paradox if we ceased to (mis)translate Jesus' relationship to scandal and a repressive violence that undergirds the sense of paradox utilized to justify political hierarchical relations? What alternative form of political theology might arise if we were to envision things in fact quite differently? Fundamentally, in order to answer these questions directly, we must first go through another question, one more central to theological method: what exactly is the relationship between paradox and dialectics?

For Adorno, who makes this clear in his articulation of the methods active within the negative dialectics he espouses,

> Dialectics as a philosophical mode of proceeding is the attempt to untie the knot of paradoxicality by the oldest means of enlightenment: the ruse. Not by chance has the paradox been the decaying form of dialectics from Kierkegaard on. Dialectical reason follows the impulse to transcend the natural context and its delusion (a delusion continued in the subjective compulsion of the rules of logic) without forcing its own rule upon this context—in other words, without sacrifice and without vengeance.[34]

Dialectics such as this will eventually, he conjectures, pass away, because it cannot maintain "its delusion" of succeeding with the ruse that it can proceed without imposing violent sacrifices and vengeance in the contexts within which it imposes itself. To do this is to consistently, perhaps even unconsciously, perform a (subjective) logic of identity formation that Adorno's negative dialectics—a form of "nonidentity thinking"—rejected.[35] I would only add that this seems as well to be one of the major implications for Girardian thought that is routinely understated, if not missed altogether: the intense relationship between sacrificial violence and the politics of identity formation and (normative) order. Such a connection is indeed the conclusion reached through noting the cohesion of boundaries (i.e., definitions) as what inevitably follows from the provocation of scandal.

What Adorno works toward is a reading of the absolute "as it hovers before metaphysics," as "the nonidentical that refuses to emerge until the compulsion of identity has dissolved."[36] In the renunciation of the compulsion to know who is guilty and who innocent, who the friend and who the enemy, we are released from the need to exhaustively identify anyone or anything, and so likewise freed to accept that which appears to us as existing without definition. The next "negative" step taken in negating the politics of identity formation is that which leads away from dialectics and paradox and toward the undoing of identity that becomes a form of nonidentity, what will be the central methodological process of a "negative dialectics."

In truth, however, it is *another* paradox that results from this state of things, though this one is fundamentally different, Adorno claims, from its Kierkegaardian predecessor, which had sought reductionistically to unite time with eternity.[37] This coincidence of time and eternity is itself a short-circuiting of the dynamics that refuse to act so reductively in order to legitimate a given identity or norm. What I believe Adorno was actually after would be something more like the division of time itself so that something *beyond* time—though perhaps not necessarily the eternal—might enter, what Agamben has explicitly called in a Pauline context the "time that remains."[38]

To simply unite time and eternity, or the finite and the infinite, is to establish a paradox that can be, in turn, utilized to justify a number of other reductionistic representations (as through historical uses of the "analogy of being," for example). This was Adorno's fear and what he sensed actively at work behind theological uses of paradox: that they were a reinstitution of identity and a backdoor entrance for all-too-human legitimations of power and knowledge. They hold forth the tempting possibility to form a harmonious whole when no such totality was actually possible, because no "paradoxical" balance between opposed ends could ever fully arrive at a cohesive identity.[39] In his words, "Denying the mystery by identification, by ripping more and more scraps out of it, does not resolve it. Rather, as though in play, the mystery belies our control of nature by reminding us of the impotence of our power."[40] It is only through an intentional movement downward, one made toward further weakness or impotence, and away from the violence and sacrifice that underlie dialectical movements (even if they go by the label of "paradox"), that we are able to find a solution to this problematic impasse. It is in this place, I would argue, that we might begin to formulate something like a new political theology, one no longer utilized primarily to legitimate a status quo through its articulation of paradoxical doctrinal positions.

The Political Stakes of Paradox

I would like to reframe the discussion of paradox at this point by focusing on how a related abstraction has been dealt with, and by the same thinkers as those who wish to determine the nature of paradox in strictly theological terms. By shifting our language for a moment from paradox to the exception, I believe that we might begin to see political implications that are typically not so obvious within theological propositions. For example, Carl Schmitt famously opens his discussion of political theology with the declaration that it is the sovereign who is capable of declaring a suspension of legal rule, of defining a particular moment *as* exceptional. The sovereign—legitimated *through* paradox—stands outside the system, but is also the person who belongs entirely to it insofar as the rule of law depends on the existence of the suspension itself. In this formulation of things, there is a resonance with Kierkegaard's notions of the moment, exceptionality and paradox that are too great to ignore. There is also a resonance with Marion's attempt to reinstate knowledge by using paradox to outline the limits of what we do not know.

Schmitt, for his part, makes clear that modern (liberal) constitutional thought has tried to eliminate this specific function of the sovereign, and, along with this figure, the state of emergency that had characterized the sovereign's coming to power under the conditions of paradox. He realizes, of course, that such efforts have perhaps not fully succeeded in ridding our world of its foundations in exceptionality. Indeed, it would rather seem that we *cannot* rid ourselves of such states of exception, though, in reality, we rely upon them to found our political communities and identities. There is in this insistence upon the primacy of exclusion (emergency or suspension) another resonance with Girardian thought, in that the very fabric of communal identity is predicated upon its ability to found itself upon an exclusive act (or decision) no matter how arbitrary or violent it is. It is the act of exclusion itself that constructs the community's identity and so this violent act must be considered as foundational.

What Schmitt effectively does is to politicize Kierkegaard's metaphysical description of the exception (and paradox) that Christ is, in an effort to demonstrate how the exception is more important than the rule.[41] This translation was what lay behind his assertion that all political concepts are secularized theological ones.[42] And yet, he will also assert, there must be a rule that is founded upon such a state of exception; this is the nature of a fully formed political theology. Any movement to form a state beyond "modern constitutional thought" will have to achieve its results, not solely through philosophical or political thought, but through what he terms "metaphysical conviction"—a proposition that might sound theologically satisfactory if its historical involvement with National Socialism were not so absolutely horrifying.[43]

The problem with such metaphysical speculation and its accompanying convictions, according to Agamben's reading of Schmitt on the state of exception (and as a problem that no doubt lingered in Schmitt's personal affiliation with National Socialism), occurs when the exception *becomes* the rule, that is, when an individual, acting as sovereign, attempts to turn the "zone of indistinction" that most accurately characterizes this state into a permanent rule. To engage in such a transformation is, by Agamben's count, when such a state "transforms itself into a killing machine."[44] What we should be after, Agamben counters, is rather a refusal (like Herman Melville's character of "Bartleby the Scrivener," or of a Christ-like figure not necessarily inscribed within an ecclesial context[45]) of this transformation from the state's potentiality to its actuality—a process paralleled by the movement from a negative, spectral proposition to a positive, concrete, and political one. Rather, humanity must attempt to foster a state of exception that does not seek to transform itself into a governing state that must legitimize the violence necessary to maintain its rule. Agamben's project, in sharp contrast to Schmitt's, is to bring about a dis-enchantment that does not "restore the enchanted thing to its original state"—an act of *profanation*, then, that takes us deeper into the well of our potentiality beyond any (political) representation we might be able to establish and as an entirely negative methodology that might "rightly" be mistaken, as was Derrida's, as a form of atheism.[46]

Agamben's insistence upon formulating a space for an exception that does not become the rule is not to suggest that all forms of government, religious community, or given identity are to be eradicated once and for all—a common misreading of his position in light of claims made about the "end of metaphysics" and the "death of God." The effort that Agamben puts forth to acknowledge the decline of metaphysical structures while also keeping a critical distance from embracing any actually existing structure often gives a somewhat misleading impression. His stance is rather one of reformulating the essential relationship between any established structures and identities and the negative, critical position that always accompanies them. Following in the wake of Heidegger, however, he is highly attentive to the negative dimensions of ontology today, which no longer bear the metaphysical-paradoxical presuppositions that had supported sovereign roles for centuries. In this sense, the Heideggerian critique of all-ontotheological, metaphysical positions and beliefs is certainly alive and well in Agamben's thought, even perhaps more so than in Heidegger's own philosophy, which allowed the latter to be seduced at times by fascist political ideologies.

Agamben's point, one that is often misread as advocating a suspension of all normative order, institutional structure, or legal code—as then itself antinomian—is that the only way to move beyond our inscription in violent matrices of power is to find a way to move backward, to regress toward our (ontological) poverty (our "pure potentiality"). In other words, he is seeking, not a reestablishment of sovereign rule, but the capacity to live a "form-of-life" that does not seek to possess the order that governs it. This is what he discovers in, among other places, the issues embodied historically in the Franciscan order and its renunciation of both possessions and identities. The radicality of the Franciscan renunciation of possessions is of apiece with the quest to locate a force *beyond* sovereign power as a possible basis for grace to enter our world. If seen from this angle, I believe this formulation of relations would also be parallel to Žižek's claim that Christianity is itself constituted on an exception, an "unfathomable divine mystery," which establishes human rationality, though only insofar as one realizes the weakness (and not the sovereignty) of the God who institutes it: "It is only the exception which allows us to perceive the miracle of the universal rule."[47] But in this case, since brought about through weakness and not the strength of sovereign power, such a case would differ dramatically from the exceptions, formed precisely as paradoxes, that sustain sovereign rule. How such a consideration is capable of redefining paradox itself is the question we still have to pursue in order to follow those political theologians who seek a second negation in order to avoid the ideological problematics that follow every potential negative theology.

The Kierkegaardian Move

One aspect of the paradox of faith, as we are told in Kierkegaard's *Fear and Trembling*, is that the singular individual is higher than the universal ethical system, and a teleological suspension of any ethical system follows from this existence of an unmediated faith *as* eternal paradox and as the establishment of an absolute relation to the absolute only through such a paradox.[48] Faith, then, *is* this paradox embodied. This description of faith is the crux of Kierkegaard's declaration elsewhere, contra his reading of Hegel, that truth is a form of subjectivity, one that is capable of holding together the paradox of a form of inwardness as truth and an external, objective uncertainty.[49] That the eternal truth dwells within time, within the individual, must always and only be a paradoxical state of dwelling *in* faith *on* that which is ultimately absurd, and it is this exception to objective systematic thought that grants humanity the Christian "truth," as he portrayed matters.[50]

Kierkegaard's contention was that Hegelian speculation—the system that seeks only to *know* and not, through recognition of the individual who believes, to *exist*—kills the paradox, and so kills any possibility for genuine faith. The question to put to Kierkegaard on this matter, however, is to what degree does he manage to, through trying to escape the system altogether, end up reinstituting sovereign power within the individual Christian who must now stand alone, defiantly, in a permanent critique of all existing structures (what he often termed "Christendom") that can never live up to the exceptional status of faith. In this highly Protestant formulation, Christ's very nature as the exception would seem to doom from the start any and all attempts to found a "rule" or system upon this exception housed solely within the individuals (or "knights") of faith. In this configuration of faith, we might begin to see why Kierkegaard's stress upon actuality and being over potentiality and thought (or speculation), and hence his preference for the decision, was so appealing to Schmitt, who took Kierkegaard's focus on the individual to the level where it rightly belonged, that of the political.[51]

The insistence that one's foundation (as the "origin" of faith) rests upon an unmediated experience of paradox subjectively related within the individual becomes not only a justification for exceptionalism and decisionism, as it was for Schmitt who appropriated it directly for political thought, but also, as the theologian Karl Barth saw emerging from Kierkegaard's work as clearly as did Schmitt, a political conceptualization of sovereignty within the individual Christian.[52] As with Barth's insistent critique of religion (as a human institution), his stress upon the sovereignty of God and the infinite distance between that which is infinite and this world—and though there was to be an "analogy of faith" between them (one that Hans Urs von Balthasar saw as essentially another form of the "analogy of being"[53])—Kierkegaard asks for Christians to maintain a suspension of the finite world itself, the only perspective that will allow one to return to it.[54] Again, in many ways, we are returned to the contemporary debate between the radically orthodox theologian John Milbank, with his Kierkegaardian insistence on the paradox and his insistent defense of the analogy of being,[55] and the (negative) dialectical movements of the radical philosopher Slavoj Žižek, which I will explore below.

An Alternative Reading

Perhaps there is however another way to read Kierkegaard, one more in line with alternative readings of Hegel's negation of negation itself, that opens for us an alternative path to follow. I think we might be able to advance a genuinely alternative reading, in fact, by asking a straightforward question: How exactly does Kierkegaard come to the realization that it is only through such a suspension of the system that we are, so to speak, liberated? The absolute relation, he conjectures—and which should recall to our minds the absolute nature of violence, which goes unremarked here—is only brought about, not through "relating absolutely" to the absolute, but by renouncing one's relation to "relative ends." Though he will caution that this "task is ideal and perhaps is never accomplished by anyone," he is also clear that it is only through the renunciation of relative ends that one can learn to "relate oneself absolutely to the absolute and relatively to the relative."[56] This act of renunciation is what allows an individual to find the purity of will to "will one thing," though they will suffer a good deal in doing so, he also admits.[57] But how does Kierkegaard's conception of the renunciation of relative ends differ from the "negation of negation" that Hegel had himself posited as a dying to death that Christ faced through his crucifixion, and which has inspired quite a few political and liberation theologies?[58] Is there another way to read the dialectics of history other than as one that grants, in the end, a new sovereign its right to rule?

There is at least one other way to read the suspension or state of emergency that Schmitt had adopted from Kierkegaard. In particular, we might witness Walter Benjamin's interpretation, one that drew itself, in part at least, from Schmitt's work on the exception (and this despite Benjamin's dislike of Kierkegaard on the whole, which may also help us to understand his divergence from Schmitt on this matter).[59] Benjamin's reading of the exceptions present within the normative order of history, acting as ephemeral moments of reading history "against the grain," and so as the only authentic chance for actual revolutionary thought, came about not as the result of a quest for sovereign power, but as the result of a "weak messianic force" that suspends the normativity of history.[60] Such a force was one that did not seek to re-instantiate a governing order, but only to upend the current one. This was a proposition that has led to many critical speculations that such an idea is really a covert antinomianism. For Benjamin, however, it was a chance to bring "dialectics to a standstill."[61]

What does it mean to suspend the normal structure of things, and, theologically, something like the structure of the Church? Is this merely a heightened awareness of the tensions that undergird its existence, or is there a heretical antinomianism lurking beneath such suggestions? Even Derrida had rightly suspected that his own position was one to be mistaken, as so many negative theologians have been, as a heretical and antinomian one.[62] The question can easily be put to someone like Agamben as well, who follows Benjamin very closely in many respects, and yet has, perhaps more hermeneutically than some might have suspected, at times advocated a permanent tension between the weak messianic forces working within history and the structures of law and normativity as the only possible solution to this aporia.[63] I believe that this theoretical conclusion is also what has motivated political theologians from Johann Baptist Metz to Lieven Boeve to read religion as a form of interruption—what can be seen as a helpful "corrective" to the subjects and institutions of Christianity, but not necessarily to the actual message and content of the Christian faith.[64]

The question on method that I am posing, one that is terribly difficult to sort out in theoretical terms, but which is still central to the legacy of any political theology that would nonetheless hold itself in tension with the structures of doctrine or the original Christian proclamation that ceaselessly upends our representations of God, is how are we to consider the "negation of negation" with regard to normative structures, that is, insofar as we are often presented, through the negation of identity alone, with what appears to be "an exception to the 'normal' dialectical movement"?[65] How are we also to envision this as a possible form of hypernomianism that pushes us beyond what we see before us while also retaining a stance vis-à-vis the normative measure?

The difference between such a negation of what appeared to be normative and the "negation of negation" itself, following Žižek's reading of Hegel, is that it is only the second negation that can reveal the precariousness of normativity itself. The truly Hegelian dialectical movement is one that preserves the qualities of what it negates within itself, not simply presenting us with an overcoming of them in a wholly new synthetic union of the two.[66] Rather than merely negating any thesis with its antithesis, the thesis is actually preserved within the antithesis which then, when attempting to negate what was repressed within itself, comes to establish its subjectivity, but in such a way that any subjectivity established as such is, more or less, a "nonidentity," or the wholescale failure of identity as it were. Functioning like Freud's "return of the repressed"—a figure very much appreciated in this context by Derrida to be sure—the negated element returns to "haunt" an established identity because it is constituent *of* the identity and can never be completely effaced. Such a reading becomes very salient in theological terms, as I will explore in a moment.

Unlike the simple negation of a positive concept, which is a singular distortion, a negation of negation recognizes how distortion within the field of one's perception is itself constitutive of any conceptualization in the first place.[67] In other words, any feigned objectivity that takes place in the awareness of distortion is brought to the level of the subjective in that it involves seeing how the subject is self-reflexively involved in the process of distortion itself. This presents us with a movement that ultimately delivers Kierkegaard's correct emphasis on subjectivity, but which also perhaps renders Kierkegaard a bit more Hegelian than he might have liked.[68]

In addition, we see a parallel formulation of this negation of negation in Agamben's reading of Pauline thought, wherein the division between spirit and flesh itself divides any other social or legal division, such as between Jew and Gentile, male and female, slave and free (as suggested in Paul's thoughts in Galatians 3:28). Since every identity, founded by a sort of legalistic social or political representation, can be further divided, we are freed in a sense from all representations, while also being still subject to them, not having externally bypassed them, but by having negated them from within.[69] This internal, messianic "division of division" itself introduces a remnant within the normative representation, one that is permanently "not all" to itself, neither wholly Jew nor wholly non-Jew. The Pauline "division of division" mirrors what takes place in the "negation of negation" in that it preserves the first term—in this case Jewishness—while also pointing out how being Jewish is no longer equal to itself: "Not all of those of Israel are Israel," as he puts it in the context of his discussion of spirit and flesh in Romans (9:6).[70] The conclusion that is reached is ultimately that weakness and vulnerability are inherent not only to Christian subjectivity but also to any representation we might give of ourselves. Christ is, as both Caputo and Žižek recognize, to be understood as a "weak" God.[71] The "Christian sublime," as Žižek will put it, is drawn toward a dialectics involving a "downward synthesis" that always gravitates toward the "lowest point at which the common ground of position and negation is worn away."[72] All that is left is a "remainder" that "falls out from the symbolic order": "the order of universal symbolic mediation as it were collapses into an inert left-over."[73] This is the "not-All" that remains after the second negation is performed on the first negation, leaving us with a permanently fractured ontology.[74] It is only from this place that we can begin to get a sense of what message any radical theology worth its salt will have to maintain in relation to traditional religious structures and institutions.

These suggestions also go some ways toward explaining why Christianity's stress upon the weakness, vulnerability, and brokenness of its deity leads almost inevitably toward Christianity's proffering a deconstruction of itself, as Jean-Luc Nancy, among others, has suggested.[75] There is an inevitable turn from these Christian claims regarding subjectivity to the deconstruction of subjectivity itself. The Western subject, formed in the crucible of the Christian tradition, is thereby forced to reckon with its deconstruction at its own hands, allow (post)modern critiques of the subject, psychoanalytic critiques of the self and secular criticism of religious identity all to flourish as the outcomes of Christian claims, not simply as their oppositional partners. In other words, Christianity's deconstruction is brought about by Christianity itself, by elements working within it that actually mirror the self-deconstructing deity that it worships. This truth is what will allow us to recognize that there is no firm boundary between self-reflexive religious impulses and the nature of philosophical reflection, much as Marcel Gauchet has affirmed in his study of secularism that runs parallel to Nancy's.[76]

This line of thought in particular will result in Žižek's defense of a sort of "poverty of God," in that he searches for a demonstration of how God has nothing but God's own being to give to humanity, that which was given to creation itself so that it might exist in the first place.[77] This formulation, I would only further note, is strikingly parallel to Agamben's "Franciscan" ontology that likewise points toward the poverty of ontology itself, how it pours itself out in the fracturing of any representation that it might attempt to give of itself. Again, we are following a path opened up by the "end of metaphysics" and its accompanying paradoxes that Heidegger has once pointed out so rigorously, but we are also more capable than Heidegger of seeing how this critical path implicates every self who would extend its critical gaze, not simply outward, but primarily inward.

What Agamben's unfolding of this Pauline logic specifically points toward is what Žižek outlines as the real objective of Hegelian dialectics: the goal is neither to produce a third, synthetic term nor to strike a balance between thesis and antithesis; it is rather to "recognize in one pole the symptom of the failure of the other."[78] As Žižek continues, "The solution is to revolutionize or change the universal term itself [...] so that it will no longer require its symptom as the guarantee of its unity."[79] No longer would the Jew need the non-Jew to identify itself, so long as the Jew was revolutionized from within, divided internally from themselves, and so able to see their own failure to "be Jewish" as the only possible resolution of one's identity (again, as a "nonidentity" in Adorno's parlance, and as we will see in the next chapter).[80] Another way of saying this, one that resonates a good deal with the contemporary reformulations of political theology I have been following—Adorno, Agamben, Žižek, and even Judith Butler included—is that the only genuine way to represent something is by showing your failure to represent it. In this sense, the negation of negation functions as a "failed negation" wherein, in Žižek's words, "the subject separates itself from its symbolic representations."[81]

Hence, Žižek will himself follow a variety of thinkers who have noted how Christianity appears to be the first religion to demystify the sacred, something that certainly introduces another sense of paradox into the central message of Christianity and its portrayals of sacrality.[82] Other senses of Christian paradox, ones markedly divergent from those utilized to justify the re-entrance of sovereign power, emerge in Žižek's thought and could also be considered as staging points for this conceptualization. As he will (re)define paradox in his *Absolute Recoil*: "What the position of Christian doubt involves is a pragmatic paradox succinctly rendered by Alyosha in Dostoyevsky's *The Brothers Karamazov*: 'God exists but I am not sure whether I believe in Him,' where 'I believe in Him' refers to the believer's readiness to fully assume the existential engagement implied by such a belief [...]"[83]; or, later in the same book, "freedom is impossible, but it is also impossible to escape it and put all the blame on Fate," what he considers a "paradox that defines the non-All [...]"[84]; or, when he discusses the paradox of there being no subject prior to the gap, or self-alienation, that constitutes the subject[85]; or, in what will be perhaps the greatest paradox for the future of belief itself, the atheist who, through the negation of negation, is capable of preserving faith—not as a "negative" theology, equated with believing in an "un-God"—but as a belief without belief in any "Big Other," an "unbelief" perhaps somewhat close to Caputo's (and Derrida's) rendering of a "religion without religion."[86] The *paradoxical* conclusion for Žižek in the end is ultimately that "[...] atheism is the secret inner conviction of believers who externalize their belief, while belief is the secret inner conviction of public atheists."[87]

In these formulations we are not very far, I would suggest, from Halík's obviously much more pastorally minded considerations of how the believer and the atheist overlap a good deal while waiting in patience before each other. There is a translation that takes place between the experience of the believer and the experience of the non-believer that seeks not to reduce the identity of the one for the other. There is rather a non-reductive exchange made possible through the self-imposed division of each side by its own hand, resulting in an act that allows each side to "reach" the other through the dissolution of whatever identity had appeared to undergird its sense of self. In other words, the marginalized and radical elements of any given group will be able to recognize themselves in the faces of the orthodox, and the orthodox will be able to see themselves present in the faces of the radicals.

In these considerations of paradox, Žižek will also endorse René Girard's thesis against sacrificial violence, mentioning Girard by name and concluding that the logic of the "non-All," the outcome of a negation of negation, involves a sacrifice (of Christ) intended to bring an end to "the very logic of sacrifice."[88] Žižek even points directly in this context toward the "death of God" that takes place in Jesus' death on the cross as the "tragic *skandalon* of the Christian experience," *the* result of the negative dialectics that Christianity elevates above all else to a principle of nonidentity.[89] This is the "way of the Cross" that cannot be located within an abstract theological reversion to harmonious beauty (what Žižek sees operative in John Milbank's work). In this way, Žižek finds another, more traumatic paradox in Kierkegaard's characterization, one located more in our human failings (his reading of Kierkegaard's "sickness unto death") rather than solely in the merger of the eternal with time.[90] This is a conclusion that I would suggest lies much closer to the Kantian version of the sublime than it does to any description of the beautiful. As God takes the act of negation upon God's own self, resulting in the "death of God," God is likewise "personalized," or brought to the level of subjectivity, insofar as

God presses beyond all knowledge and toward a sublime paradox bound up within human existence to be sure.

The Political Theological Implications of Paradox

So where does this leave us regarding the role of paradox within Christian proclamation? And where does our (in)ability to deal with paradox in light of a certain negative dialectics leave us with regard to the future of political theology? In response to the first question, the paradoxes that undergird the Christian narrative—from the Incarnation to God's death on the cross, and so speaking directly to the atheist within the believer and the believer within the atheist—must be central to the establishment of one's faith and (non)identity as a Christian, but only insofar as such a position is staked out on the terrain of an increasingly bold movement toward one's own poverty, toward the failure of one's identity, even and especially as a "Christian." That is, the more one believes, the more one is inclined to see where it is that they do not believe, making very realistic the position for faith that repeatedly exclaims: "Lord, I believe; help my unbelief" (Mark 9:24).

To be clear, I do not think that Halík's position, or Žižek's or Agamben's, among others, is a liminal one, resting on an ambiguous middle ground between belief and unbelief. To suggest this is to suggest as well that Paul was trying to formulate something like a liminal identity between the Jew and the Greek—one that most likely arose as a misreading of Pauline theology at a gathering of apostles in Jerusalem long ago (see Acts 15 and Galatians 2). What is rather being advocated, I think, is the suspension of identity itself through a type of negative dialectics, a "negation of negation," or "division of division" that is predicated upon the failure of identity, not a vague search for a third identity (as is common in certain misreadings of Hegelian dialectics as well). That is, even the identity of the Jew is divided from within, into spirit and flesh, a further division of an existing social division that effectively undoes the first division without actually eradicating it altogether. It is with this understanding that Paul could be a Jew with other Jews and a Gentile with other Gentiles, but not be what we today would consider to be a relativist (1 Corinthians 9:20-23). If we can see this dynamic unfolding before our eyes as such, it is the source of a grace lived beyond any law, Wolfson's position of "hypernomianism" or Agamben's quest for a form-of-life lived beyond the law.

With regard to the future of political theology, much more remains to be said. At the least, and despite the increasingly complex refinements of what exactly takes place in a negative dialectical movement that undergirds Pauline theology, there is very little we can assert in the end that is new, other than the increased realization that there will always be tensions between structures (or traditions) and "weak" messianic experiences that undo the former, only to watch them be rebuilt again. This is a point that I believe, and despite their apparent radicality and difference from each other, figures as diverse as Derrida and Agamben both end up ultimately endorsing.

The temptation to resist for the theologian, however, is one that would seek to restore a sovereign (metaphysical, ontotheological) position, whether in the institution of the Church, the papacy, the nation-state or its "sovereign," the individual believer or any other object that we can potentially infuse with such an illusion. This fetish of theology, as I would call it, to regain a place of prominence within either society, academy, or the Church, must be continuously sought out and named for what it is: a distraction from the "downward synthesis" or poverty of identity that Christians are rather called to seek after, even to the point of the dissolution of their own identities and the embrace of what may appear as a form of atheism.[91]

In this way perhaps too we are given a new perspective on any possible tension between heresy and orthodoxy, as heresy is in actuality a constitutive part of the "orthodox" identity, or any identity for that matter. It remains, as it were, a permanent temptation that humanity must repeatedly face as part of the generation of any (orthodox) identity, not as an obstacle that is to be permanently overcome so that a stronger identity might be asserted. Moving beyond simply an ecclesial context even, humanity must find the heretical *within* the orthodox, and the orthodox *within* the heretical, allowing both discoveries to ultimately "undo" us.

Parallel to this suggestion lies another, that the perceived fracture between the sacred and the secular, as between the believer and the atheist, is a false dichotomy. Rather than opt for one over the other, the real challenge before humanity is to see how both can be divided from within, revealing a much more fragile sense of identity that might be more profitably deconstructed as well. Traditionally, the sacred has been understood as a suspension of the normal state of things, of the everyday use of things that has now been reserved for special, sacred use. If we are to learn anything from the Christian narrative of God's death on the cross, however, theologians must be aware that such a death brings about the "alienation of our alienation," as Jürgen Moltmann once put it, through God's alienation from God's own self—a double movement that makes real, once again, the negation of negation so essential to theological method.[92] For his part, Agamben will read this act of double alienation as the ultimate profanation of the sacred, a move which, in Žižek's opinion, is really the same zero-level equivalent of sacralization.[93] Whatever it ends up being in the end, I would think, will be most profitable for political theology to consider, for it will hold the fate of the field as a whole for some time to come.

2

Negation

Theologians are often beset by the difficulties encountered in modern forms of critical thought and the postmodern demise of grand narratives, or at least this is how the situation is often perceived and frequently portrayed.[1] The (post)modern shift in theological thought, on the whole made in an effort to cope with such problematics and to preserve a viable notion of the paradox as we have just seen, has at least since the criticisms of figures as diverse as Spinoza and Heidegger inclined many to tilt toward an enclosed plane of immanence rather than attempt to reconstruct an ontotheological justification for sovereign forms of transcendence. This is a move that perhaps makes more sense to us at this point in our analysis of possible theological resistances to sovereign power cloaked in negative theological guises.[2] Traditionally understood, ontotheology has been in decline ever since these modern champions of immanence, though its alleged and so-called death is something that remains to be determined. As Adorno himself had once famously suggested, "After Auschwitz there is no word tinged from on high, not even a theological one, that has any right unless it underwent a transformation."[3] Constructing a form of transcendence through recourse to traditional notions of paradox in order to undergird one's theological point of view has been typically little more than a ploy for political power, whether ecclesial, social, or personal in nature, and immanence has often been criticized by political theologians defending such moves as a form of antinomian rhetoric bent on displacing those in positions of power.

In this (post)modern theological displacement and reconfiguration, the critique of the ways in which theology has traditionally perceived its (transcendent) object of study has made things much more restrictive in terms of positive constructs offered, presenting us with a reality that frequently lessens the political power of religious institutions in the West and consequently pits a defensive and apologetic form of theology that would defend the sovereignty of the divine, and its support through a paradoxical logic, against an increasingly liberal and secular society (and even the occasional, if seemingly contradictory, "secular" or "radical" theology). If there is to be a hope for theological reflection in the near future, it must take Adorno's suggestion—inasmuch as it also echoes a sentiment found in Dietrich Bonhoeffer's later work—quite seriously: theology must be transformed or it will no longer be able to speak to our world in a meaningful way. Within such a context, I believe that Adorno's intuition for developing a theology post-Auschwitz as noted above is entirely correct. I believe as well that we are still trying to work out the implications of what all of this means for theological methods and models, hence the need to clarify the types of paradox operative within theology's history.

The lines, moreover, between theology and philosophy continue to be blurred in this regard, playing out Adorno's suggestion, made in his *Negative Dialectics*, that "[…] transcendence feeds on nothing but the experiences we have in immanence,"[4] though what this entails exactly is still somewhat unclear. Through a look at the relationship between transcendence and immanence, as well as between the sacred and the secular, we might nevertheless be able to deduce the dialectics of negation as they provide another way to perceive how a negative dialectics might aid theological reflection in the future.

Transcendence as the Failure of Immanence

From the beginning, I would suggest that what we are forced to contemplate in Adorno's reconceptualization of theological thought is a profound rereading of the relationship between the immanent and the transcendent, or, if you will, between the material and the theological. As he claims, "At its most materialistic, materialism comes to agree with theology. Its great desire would be the resurrection of the flesh, a desire utterly foreign to idealism, the realm of the absolute spirit."[5] Contrary to an idealistic abstraction from the material realm, Adorno hits upon that which has been, and will presumably continue to be, very fruitful for the recovery of theological insight, and in contradistinction with those metaphysical, transcendental subjectivities that have often undergirded theological projects precisely through their almost complete abstraction from the conditions of material reality. As the German political theologian Jürgen Moltmann would put it in light of Adorno's work, the resurrection of the flesh matters in a way that theology has often neglected to comprehend:

> To recognize the event of the resurrection of Christ is therefore to have a hopeful and expectant knowledge of this event. It means recognizing in this event the latency of that eternal life which in the praise of God arises from the negation of the negative, from the raising of one who was crucified and the exaltation of the one who was forsaken.[6]

This is, in short, the negation of the ultimate immanent negation—death itself then—and it is thereby also a stress laid upon the resurrected materiality of the flesh. For Moltmann, in particular, such a suggestion eventually yields an intensified focus upon the suffering of Christ, or what was, in the end, and following Martin Luther's phrasing, the "Crucified God."[7] As the negation of the negative, this form of negative dialectics would, in his eyes, open theology up to the reality of suffering in a way that theology had not been attentive to prior to the horrors of Auschwitz. Such a movement was not an idealistic dialectics that sought to remove itself from material reality, but a negative dialectics that would return to the material reality beyond whatever label had been inscribed over it.

It was precisely this return to our material realities which had led Adorno to state that "the smallest trace of senseless suffering in the empirical world belies all the identitarian philosophy that would talk us out of that suffering: 'While there is a beggar, there is a myth,' as Benjamin put it. This is why the philosophy of identity is the mythological form of thought."[8] Suddenly, from this perspective, demythologization becomes a theological task, though one that differs from Rudolf Bultmann's efforts, and which likewise differs from traditional theological projects working in league with a certain history of metaphysics sustained on political notions of paradox. In a way that would open theology up to its more contextual, emancipatory projects (e.g., liberation, black, feminist, postcolonial, and queer theologies, among others), Adorno's insight offers us a way to see how the theological must be understood in relation to its material realities and traditions. There is a potential "theological materialism," as Patrice Haynes has put things, latent within Adorno's work, though it is one that also retains a certain paradoxical nature, and, as such, might be seen to maintain a so-called heretical position, not in the least because he also declares that the core of religion is, and should remain, empty.[9]

This call to perceive religious "truth" as a contentless vessel of human experience and understanding is actually a call that has been made repeatedly in certain (post)modern circles of contemporary philosophy of religion. From Derrida to Caputo and Benjamin to Agamben, theology should be said to work less in the interest of preserving its traditions and doctrines, and more in service to a "weak messianic force" that moves throughout any and every tradition, promising justice and truth to shine forth, though it is also often misperceived as an antinomian or heretical force when it is most loyal to its core intentions. The real "deposit of faith," however, is perhaps a gesture toward something we have not yet grasped, and perhaps never will in its entirety. The logic of the (negative) weak messianic force dictates that this must be so.

What is most interesting in this particular reading of religion is that, despite religion being declared fundamentally empty content-wise, from this point of view it still maintains a "more consistent" form of materiality than those metaphysical positions which were developed in conjunction with theological claims (i.e., the long history of Western ontotheology so often decried). Religion maintains, as it were, something intrinsic to its hope that is nonetheless essential to the project of negative dialectics, though this is only, at times, hinted at by Adorno:

> Christian dogmatics, in which the souls were conceived as awakening simultaneously with the resurrection of the flesh, was metaphysically more consistent—more enlightened, if you will—than speculative metaphysics, just as hope means a physical resurrection and feels defrauded of the best part by its spiritualization. With that, however, the impositions of metaphysical speculation wax intolerably.[10]

Seen as such, the belief in a physical resurrection takes the nature of materiality more seriously than subsequent metaphysical speculation and its spiritualization of a theological materiality which, for its part, should not be discarded in such a manner. The faults of idealism are again on display as Adorno suggestively points toward a material theology that has long been ignored, but which is essential to any traditional theological foundation for belief. Though Adorno is not necessarily looking to defend religious doctrine, we see what distance separates Adorno's project of demythologization from

Bultmann's, which would jettison the physical resurrection as an inherently "mythological" element of the Gospel accounts and so expose its own existentialist metaphysical supports.

What Adorno is ultimately after is of course no less radical than Bultmann's claims, though on a level altogether different. What Adorno gestures toward is a subversion of those religious-ideological identities that have been politically staked, but which are rarely useful in any genuinely theological sense: "The idea of truth is supreme among the metaphysical ideas, and this is where it takes us. It is why one who believes in God cannot believe in God, why the possibility represented by the divine name is maintained, rather, by him who does not believe."[11] What is present in his thought is precisely, and as we saw already in Žižek's contrast of the believer and the atheist, that which appears to be not present—an identity only suggested through one's nonidentity, what Emmanuel Levinas had once referred to as the form of a "relation without relation" (and which became the basis for Derrida's later adaptation of a "religion without religion").[12] I would wager that such considerations are not too far removed either from figures such as Derrida and Caputo who seem to revel in these reversals of identity, or from believers who rightly pass for atheists.[13]

The reference to Derrida in this context might also help to make clearer how a great deal of frustration has often been on display in response to those deconstructive (or negative dialectical) projects that refuse to engage in a "positive" political or identitarian project. This refusal, for instance, was what had made the discussion of paradox in relation to ideology in the last chapter so difficult to discern. Along these lines of inquiry, the very real question many would put to Adorno in this context, as it might and often was to Derrida, is: should we resist this "non-identity" as the only solution to the problem of identity, as Patrice Haynes again has suggested, trying instead to assert a more "positive ontology" in the face of this loss?[14] And yet as Adorno had perhaps already answered this presupposing question: "[…] the fallacy is the direct elevation of negativity, the critique of what merely is, into positivity as if the insufficiency of what is might guarantee that what is will be rid of that insufficiency. Even *in extremis* a negated negative is not a positive."[15]

In tones that will echo within the deconstructivist project itself centered on a justice always yet "to come" but never fully present in the future—in fact dependent upon an eschatological horizon of justice that could never be present in its entirety, for this would be the perpetually unrealized myth of totalitarianism—negative dialectics does not "rest in itself, as if it were total. This is its form of hope."[16] In sharp contrast to metaphysical-mythological, "enlightened" thought, such a messianic focus upon a future horizon always yet to come exhibits an altogether different way to envision the theological elements always already *within* our world, the broaching of the mythical immanent sphere with *something like* transcendence, though not a form of transcendence we have ever seen before. It is one that must be embodied, hence Adorno's stress on a "physical resurrection." It is a transcendence present only in the *failure* of the immanent. In other words, it is that which shines through an (immanent) negation *of* the immanent which exists *as* a negation of anything that might lie beyond it. Only through this understanding can Adorno declare that the only solidarity that exists between thinking and metaphysics exists "at the time of its fall."[17] In other words, the only genuine representation is one that is capable of showing us the failure of our representations. As I had indicated earlier, this is the only way to comprehend or perceive a true presentation beyond representation as something of a genuine possibility: the negation of representation, the negation of that which had already negated (or perhaps simply *reduced*, as the phenomenologists might say) a possible presence in our world. This is the only way by which we might access something like a true hypernomianism that refrains from actually becoming a much-feared, and much-maligned, antinomian (or nihilistic) stance.[18]

The Assault against Mythology

The entirety of Adorno's negative dialectics seems to revolve around this central pivot: thought itself is broached by that which negates it, but which, by that very negation, gives renewed life to it. Or, more directly stated, "Represented in the inmost cell of thought is that which is unlike thought."[19] We are brought back as such to the foundations of Adorno's negative dialectics, which posits that "immanence is the totality of those identitarian positions whose principle falls before immanent critique."[20] In other words, "No immanent critique can serve its purpose wholly without outside knowledge, of course—without a moment of immediacy, if you will, a bonus from the subjective thought that looks beyond the dialectical structure."[21] This is an immediacy, of course, that comes as well only from the failures of mediation, but it is the very immediacy that also undoes what we had strived so hard to uphold as an identity in the first place.

It is from this site that we begin to understand why Adorno could only construct his post-Auschwitz philosophy as a particular "logic of disintegration" or a philosophy in fragments, notions both akin to Johann Baptist Metz's political-theological suggestion that "systematic" reflections are no longer possible as certain figures of the Enlightenment might have attempted them.[22] What is left in their stead is a firm call for a philosophy of self-reflection—a "thinking against itself" (much as Rosemary Radford Ruether had once tried to discern a Church "against itself") with dire implications for those un-self-reflective philosophies that depict grand systems.[23] This refusal of systematic identity is ultimately what motivates Adorno's negative dialectics and what perhaps precipitates new thoughts within Maurice Blondel's theological speculations as well (which I will take up in a moment): a theology that thinks against itself, and which must therefore begin thinking with, and *within*, immanence in order to think toward, but not necessarily arrive at, an ephemeral moment of transcendence. To see things as such becomes another way to champion a theology that dares *to think the non-theological*, perhaps even the philosophical, just as the philosophical must think the non-philosophical, *perhaps even the theological*. To envision relations between such fields as inherently porous like this—and so to practice the only form of paradox that refuses to become possessive—is to expose the *myth* of the closed (entirely immanent) systematic reflection. This proposition, of course, is the real myth that Adorno, along with Max Horkheimer, had once sought to dispel.

In their co-authored *Dialectic of Enlightenment*, for example, we hear these two prominent critical theorists suggest that "the principle of immanence, the explanation of every event as repetition, which enlightenment upholds against mythical imagination, is that of myth itself."[24] In this formulation, events are perceived as repetitive, or cyclical, because the wholly immanent system cannot admit anything beyond itself, cannot open itself up to that which is other to it, to that which speaks another language, or is foreign to its particular paradigm. Everything seeks a stasis that cannot be upended by the intrusion of a "foreign" element: "Hence, for both mythical and enlightened justice, guilt and atonement, happiness and misfortune, are seen as the two sides of an equation. Justice gives way to law," and the entire cyclical phenomenon has begun again.[25] Though this may appear as a "modern" conceptualization through its equating the logic of enlightenment with the oldest of mythological devices, we can also observe how the tension between justice and law is continuously maintained in religious circles today at all costs, with the one frequently, even paradoxically, flowing into the other. Though there is certainly a biblical precedent for this tension, there is also no easy—often wrongly "Christianized"—solution to it. The one does not supersede the other, and the two do not always balance one another out—or, at least, balancing them is not the point they are trying to achieve in relation to one another. This truth is no less present in Girard's critique of the violence of mythology as it is here in Adorno's and Horkheimer's reflections.[26]

For Pauline thought, the tension between the law and grace (or Gospel) is paramount to comprehending the essential core of the Christian proclamation. Just as with the spirit/flesh dichotomy that subdivides the Jewish identity from within, we have in Adorno's estimation a similar dialectic of nonidentity as the only, and justly, sought-after identity, one that does not become a "positive" identity in its own right. Again, I would point out, this is what Moltmann has described in a theological context as a form of the "negation of negation"—a consideration he derives, in part, from Adorno's reflections on negative dialectics: "Out of the night of the 'death of God' on the cross, out of the pain of the negation of himself, he is experienced in the resurrection of the crucified one, in the negation of the negation, as the God of promise, as the coming God."[27] This is, for Moltmann, the only form of a positive statement that can be made. As it was for Adorno, then, to seek a positive ontology is to capitulate to identitarian thought, and to posit—through recourse to a sovereign paradox—some type of an ideological identity instead.[28]

I would only hasten to add to this connection the Pauline "division of division itself" in the commentaries of Agamben, as we saw earlier, who likewise seeks to avoid any positive content being given to identity.[29] With a certain equivalence to Adorno's comments on religion, Agamben too determines the shape of a potential theology transformed from within by its own radical messianic impulses. For him, there is no positive doctrinal content to point toward, only the "division of division" that signals a certain nonidentity which must nevertheless be respected—in many ways, the singular point of "whatever being," or the form-of-life, where ethics truly begin.[30]

To frame this movement within the context of Adorno's critique of mythology, we can see how it is mythology—which historically has often masqueraded within and as theology—that promotes a facile and ideological form of unity beyond division, a solitary, sovereign sense of an undivided self. As such, the task of rendering the subject divided from within is an ethical task of the highest order. It must be denounced again and again: "Demythologization is division; the myth is the deceptive unity of the undivided."[31] For this reason, the mythology which enlightened thinking promotes—a quest to purify itself of all myth, and to remain forever undivided from within, which is the ultimate myth—is in many ways the greatest and most deceptive myth of all, the one that both philosophy and an able political theology should seek to dismantle in its political, religious, and philosophical guises.

The Poverty of Theology

In the theologian Maurice Blondel's language, to think oneself free of all superstitions is the ultimate superstition—it is the myth of having no myths that binds one even more tightly to myth than one might think imaginable.[32] It is the modern, enlightened quest to purify oneself of all forms of idolatry, or of those fetishes, that ensures that one is doubly, though unconsciously, ensnared within them. This is a point too that certainly echoes well with Adorno's treatment of the fetish on several counts.[33] Whether we radicalize Blondel's method of immanence in a theological-phenomenologically way, as both Emmanuel Falque and Jean-Luc Marion have sought to do, in order to focus on the body "from below" so as to make the movement "from time to eternity,"[34] or whether we follow Adorno's social critique and emphasis upon suffering from a theological point of view, as both Moltmann and Metz have already done,[35] we are forced by each of these perspectives to search through the enclosures of immanence for its failings, and only from this point are we able, perhaps, to glimpse something of that which transcends the immanent plane (as with those who see the only accurate representation as the one that shows its failure to accurately represent). It is in this way that we confront what Hent de Vries has referred to, in the context of Adorno's work, as a "minimal theology," a title that plays upon Adorno's own *Minima Moralia*.[36] Such a label certainly gives one the impression that theology has lost something of its strength and that its content has been emptied of its vitality through this encounter with poetry and the limitations of language. Though in such a weakening, there is another strength humanity has yet to "identify with," which we seemingly always have trouble "identifying with" and which constitutes the real difficulty of taking religious claims seriously, because of this demand they make upon us to leave our identities behind.

To give but one example of this dynamic, we might take up the question often put to those philosophers who dabble in the principle of justice, and which is central to any analysis of alleged antinomianism: did this call for justice originate with Judaism first? Or with Christianity? As we must attentively declare, following fast on the heels of the previous chapter, the answer is both, or at least the weak messianic force that permeates them both. As de Vries considers things in the context of Adorno's work: "[…] what increasingly forces itself on our attention is that Jewish existence, in a certain sense, was paradigmatic of the 'enclaves of negation' which might authenticate the integrity of his theory."[37] In many ways, this futile quest for an origin that is really an undergirding force within all structures is similar to Derrida's and Caputo's wrestling with the "origins" of their messianic speculations. Yet, as I would also recall to mind, their views are, like Moltmann's, eschatologically oriented. It matters little what the point of origin actually is: Judaism, Christianity, or another religion that breaks into the West from elsewhere. Indeed, to search for the origins as a fixed point of orientation is an ideological task, and not a genuine theological one. A "minimal theology" is more concerned about the justice always yet to come than with the source of its foundations or a particular religious tradition from which others draw their identities. Such a minimal theology searches only for the negation of a previously established identity (the first negation of a fuller material, living reality), the division of the division of whatever identity is already before us, rather than the establishment of an originary point of access or foundation while then claiming such a point as its long sought-after identity.

In these reformulated terms, a truly minimal theology is that which is more concerned with moving from the foundations of immanence outward, *toward* the infinite, *toward* the horizon that is always yet to come, and which we might describe as transcendent yet without a foundational metaphysical, ontotheological claim. If theology is to have a future, one that learns from these mindful reflections, it can only be one that tries to locate a theology that moves out *beyond* theology, toward *that which is other to it*. This movement, and only this movement, would present a genuine poverty of theology, and perhaps also the only proper way to do theology in the first place: comparatively, inter-religiously, and in such a way as to pour itself out toward that which had at first seemed wholly other than it. This is precisely why theology, if seen from this point of view, not only has nothing to fear from modern forms of atheism; it rather seeks to pour itself out in a kenotic event that perpetually mirrors the death of God and opens the door toward the loss of any theological grounds for sovereign power.

To embrace the radical poverty of theology is, I would note moreover, to recognize that faith itself forever remains in a state of impoverishment. It is not a permanently fixed or unchallengeable entity, or institution, that is built so as to withstand its weakening; it is rather a focused look at precisely how the weakness that constitutes its core is to be understood and engaged. This, in many ways, is how we should reconceive the much maligned split between the sacred and the secular that continues to dominate our Western, religious topography. What we fail to note when we read this apparent fracture as a problem waiting to be overcome is how the divide between the sacred and the secular is not removed from the Jewish and Christian traditions, but is rather *inherent to them*. It is internal to their foundational sense of self. In particular, there is a certain "disjunction" that Christianity emphasizes in the experience of God as it comes about through God's own death that simultaneously upends our experience of ourselves, provoking a ceaseless probing of ourselves in order to ascertain how we might better betray ourselves, so to speak. This movement is, and here somewhat deepening Adorno's account above, an "immanentism of transcendence."[38]

Reconceiving of the Secular

Julia Kristeva, to take up but one significant parallel thesis within the dynamics I am addressing, becomes attuned to just such a moment in history, not simply because it defines the inner critical voice of psychoanalysis, which it does as a field that becomes for her a possible historical variant of theology,[39] but because such a disjunction in the history of the human being renders secularization almost "negligible" in the larger scheme of things.[40] It is interesting that her reading of psychoanalysis as a variant of theology runs parallel to her depiction of psychoanalysis as a possible path forward for the establishment of an "atheism without nihilism," as she phrases it.[41] Both religion and atheism, in psychoanalytic form at least, deal with the creation of symbolic, representative meaning—in other words, "a concern for coherence and identity."[42] What she touches upon most directly, we should add, is the "need to believe" that is rooted in the experience of language, a "happy infantile and amorous trauma,"[43] that stretches toward the "bonds of investment" caught up within all forms of symbolization.[44] It is not something limited to the realm of the theological, however.

Belief, for her, is an experience, not solely indebted to concepts, reasoning, historical facts or contexts, but rather an experience of truth that undergirds and sustains relations all around us. "It is a matter of a *truth* 'we stumble upon,' to which I cannot not adhere, that totally, fatally subjugates me, that I hold for vital, absolute, indisputable: *credo quia absurdam*. A truth that keeps me, makes me exist."[45] It is a Joycean "coherent absurdity" that paradoxically also takes us out of ourselves *ek-statically*.[46] It "dispossesses" a person of themselves, much as God once dispossessed God's own self *of* God through the death of

Jesus, an act that is also reminiscent of Meister Eckhart's prayer that God free us of God.[47] The resonance between Kristeva's formulations, in this regard, and the host of radical-political theologies I have been pursuing thus far should at this point be fairly obvious.

Kristeva's unique addition to this wager, however, is that in taking a deeper look at such a "pre-religious" longing to believe, we might confront both fundamentalist and secular worldviews at the same time.[48] That is, the desire to believe beyond religious forms and traditions has the possibility to introduce a new way of thinking politically that is precisely founded upon a Western, Christian way of being in the world that is also, in today's context, open to critiquing both religious and secular points of view—and as Žižek has already intimated in his work as well.[49] For Kristeva, there is a minimal theology put forth by Christianity that introduces a "sharable" form of suffering in order to provide access to our vulnerability as humans, the very thing that might bring about a new form of politics that shares with others who suffer and so is uniquely capable of speaking to a world increasingly torn apart by violence.[50] Such a theo-political point of view is only made possible by the "negative" rupture or disjunction at the heart of the Christian, universalized subject, one brought about through a kenotic form of suffering that serves to remove passion from the self, hence a "de-eroticized" suffering.[51]

I would only add that Kristeva's analysis shares to a certain degree an understanding with Charles Taylor's study of secularism in that both religious and secular viewpoints are "infected" with each other. That is, they are inextricably intertwined in such a way that a modern individual cannot sever one from the other without considerable loss to the integrity of the subject. To isolate one at the expense of the other is to reduce the complexity of faith—and of the human being—to a homogenous sense of conformity at the hands of an ultimately unjustifiable authority.[52] What Taylor, for his part, points toward is a recognition of the "ontological indeterminacy of language," a "poetic fragility" that incorporates and plays upon what comes before a given expression or identity.⁵³ From his point of view, the search to be made is for the "pagan" within the "Christian," which is an undoing of a fixed Christian identity inasmuch as it is also an entering into the complexity or "messiness" of a genuine theological hermeneutics.⁵⁴

The allowance of such complexity within a given identity is what enables Taylor to place his emphasis upon the tensions or "cross pressures" that typify late modern life, offering both "promise" and "threat" to a particular way of seeing the world.⁵⁵ Being caught between religious tradition and secularism, as between the objectivity-seeking "buffered" and contextually mired "porous" selves, is a state we should seek neither to escape nor to foreclose. What becomes clear when we contemplate the relationship of the sacred and the secular in the end is that one side, which introduces the "unthought" to a particular, established way of thinking, ceaselessly "fragilizes" the other side, and such a state of being is not to be wholly unwelcomed.⁵⁶ This particular hermeneutic is not the only reading of the possible poverty of theology, as we will see in a moment, though it is one that appears to pull the religious into the secular, and vice versa, so that we might get a better sense of what exactly is at stake in contemporary (post)modern struggles to identify the traditional political theological stakes within the game. Similar dynamics are present in the phenomenology of Jean-Louis Chrétien who, alongside Paul Ricoeur (whom we shall see later on), theorizes the "immemorial"—much as with Taylor's "unthought" or Roberto Esposito's "impolitical" element—as what is foundational to history while also standing outside of it.⁵⁷

What Taylor does not openly endorse, however, is the reality of any communal identity that is forced to acknowledge the existence of other competing traditions and communities in the quest to establish their autonomous and sovereign forms. How exactly are a religious community and the many believers who comprise it supposed to assume its shape and go about its daily life when other rival narratives external to its sense of self appear to undermine its most basic claims about the nature of reality and what lies beyond it? In other words, how does Taylor sit in relation to both the external world of competing religious claims and the internal, radical impulses that challenge any monolithic sense of communal identity and solidarity? This is the tension that I have been exploring so far, and it is one that we must continue to pursue into the divisions that characterize the social and cultural tensions between the religious and the secular.

The Radicality of the Proposition

The horizon toward which Charles Taylor's *A Secular Age* points, in constructive terms, lies in the "networks of agape" that move within those forms of life put forth by Christianity as an alternative to the world's order. Charity, he counsels, must be free to pursue "a skein of relations which link particular, unique, enfleshed people to each other, rather than a grouping of people together on the grounds of their sharing some important property [...]."[58] Love, once institutionalized, becomes corrupted, and what the institutionalization of Christianity resulted in, over the long course of the last several centuries, was what we have come to know as the modern world in which we live.[59] In short, it is precisely in the loose bonds of charity that Taylor searches for an alternative to an either/or scenario that would see the sovereign community rivaled by the secular contestation of its authority. But, we might ask, does Taylor fully escape, by merely reframing the division between the orthodox and the radical?

Though the networks of agape are in many ways the central community that Taylor wants to work toward in his study, they are also at the heart of the thesis developed by the radical Catholic priest and scholar Ivan Illich that Taylor discovered while working on *A Secular Age*.[60] He adopts Illich's reading of modernity because it illuminates his own, especially the emphasis Taylor places upon the development of those somewhat ill-conceived moral codes that developed and dominated Western life in the sixteenth and seventeenth centuries. Illich's willingness to look beyond the "necessity" of such codes and toward the phenomenon of love as taking precedence over them is what enamors Taylor to Illich's work and points toward something beyond one's adherence to moral systems governing human behavior, though it is clear that Taylor wants too to somewhat downplay Illich's radical views in the hopes of retaining the significance of the religious for the age in which we live.

Despite his adopting such a stance, however, Taylor is certainly not ignorant to the radicality of Illich's proposal, as the apparent dismantling of human moral coding in modernity is no simple task. To favor a "network of agape" over the apparent rigor and consistency of an institutionalized moral code appears to take apart what is fundamental to all forms of social and political organization—the alleged antinomian furor I have already singled out to observe and potentially reconfigure as a part of the structure itself.

> What is Illich telling us? That we should dismantle our code-driven, disciplined, objectified world? Illich was a thoroughgoing radical, and I don't want to blunt his message. I can't claim to speak for him, but this is what I draw from his work. We can't live without codes, legal ones which are essential to the rule of law, moral ones which we have to inculcate in each new generation. But even if we can't fully escape the nomocratic-judicialized-objectified world, it is terribly important to see that that is not all there is, that it is in many ways dehumanizing, alienating; that it often generates dilemmas that it cannot see, and in driving forward, acts with great ruthlessness and cruelty.[61]

What Taylor fashions alongside Illich's insights is a hermeneutics that attempts to strike a balance between the necessity of moral coding—the aptly titled "nomocratic-judicialized-objectified world"—and its undoing at the hands of those (messianic) "networks of agape" that appear to operate outside the bounds of any established morality. The possibility to counter legalistic acts of dehumanization or alienation lies within such a dialectical tension. In this sense, Taylor issues a word of caution concerning our propensity to construct moral systems:

Codes, even the best codes, can become idolatrous traps, which tempt us to complicity in violence. Illich can remind us not to become totally invested in the code, even the best code of a peace-loving, egalitarian, liberalism. We should find the centre of our spiritual lives beyond the code, deeper than the code, in networks of living concern, which are not to be sacrificed to the code, which must even from time to time subvert it. This message comes out of a certain theology, but it could be heard with profit by everybody.[62]

This is the resolution of the seemingly ever-present tension between structure and anti-structure that creeps up over and again in Taylor's analysis of modern secularity, much as it has done in Michel Foucault's genealogical work on various historical tensions.[63] It is a resolution that is really a non-resolution in that there will never be a code or an anti-code that we might permanently advance, though the temptation to divide the world up into the orthodox and the heretical antinomian will most likely persist. Humanity is always caught in-between the two poles, searching for a form of life beyond the representational tension (*the* definition of hypernomianism, as we saw in the last chapter), though just as often failing to achieve anything permanently resembling this state of being.

Illich, for his part, had described such a state of being as one that was fundamentally, in an anti-modern sense, *without* purpose and as such capable of accessing something like grace (a highly significant point that I only underscore here and will pursue later, and more directly, in the context of the sublime in Chapter 3). In Illich's estimation, modernity and its technological, instrumental rationality, issued in a replacement of the good with the valuable, a switch that immediately elevated the efficient over the purposeless:

> The valuable always implies some relationship to effectiveness, to efficiency, therefore to device, to tool, to purpose. It has become very difficult at the end of the modern time to imagine actions which are good and beautiful

without in any way being purposeful. What I meant when I spoke to you about the absence of a sense of grace referred to this absence of a sense of gratuity.[64]

To critique or reject the modern domination of the efficient and the technological is to attempt to access a state of being outside of the "system," as Illich would call it, to reside fundamentally in what is good and beautiful "without in any way being purposeful." This is precisely, I would argue, the very basis for determining our access to grace, as he suggests, by learning to view the crisis at the heart of the "system" or of reason, not as an obstacle to be overcome or a wound to be sutured, but rather as the means by which we might experience the gratuity and grace of life itself. These dynamics are what permanently link the radical to the orthodox religious, and what dictate that their union never be completely severed.

This admittance of the desire for something "deeper than the code" is moreover what makes the work of Agamben so philosophically resonate with the analyses of both Taylor and Illich. For not only does Agamben hold forth on propositions that seem to signal an almost antinomian fervor against the establishment of moral codes in the quest for a singular form of life lived beyond them but he also at times seems to point toward a hermeneutical position somewhat similar to Taylor's in that he seeks to maintain a productive tension between established structures and their (messianic) undoing. His proximity to Illich's general line of argumentation is what makes Agamben's more recent engagements with Illich himself that much more illuminating as well.

The Roots of Reformation

In his conclusive study to the *Homo Sacer* project, *The Use of Bodies*, Agamben picks up specifically on Illich's critique of the modern reduction of life to a fetishistic "scientific fact" rather than an actual way of living life, a form of life that Agamben too seeks to develop more fully as an authentic way of living the human life beyond those rules and codes that seek to normatively identify it.[65] His critical eye, in this regard, is trained toward undermining those formulations of life as being inherently sacred, but, in actuality, highly ideological—a conceptualization that has become highly politicized, but also problematic, in religious and doctrinal terms within today's global society. In this analysis, which is particularly apt for a contemporary context, "Church and lay institutions are converging today in regarding this spectral notion [of life], which can be applied in the same way to everything and nothing, as the sacred and principal object of their care, as something that can be manipulated and managed and, at the same time, defended and protected."[66] What is considered as "sacred," Agamben cautions us, can easily slip into an ideological defense of whatever position one wishes to safeguard against its "unholy" attackers—presumably through the manifestation of a paradoxical belief that asks its believers to embrace it beyond any claims made by reason.

Agamben's critique shares in his refusal of the sacred/secular dichotomy which, he avers, only perpetuates the problem that we are trying to overcome. This perspective marks his divergence from Taylor's defense of the sacred, while also offering us a more robust articulation of the same radical position that intrigued Taylor. As in his commentary elsewhere, Agamben states how "secularization is a form of repression. It leaves intact the forces it deals with by simply moving them from one place to another. Thus the political secularization of theological concepts (the transcendence of God as a paradigm of sovereign power) does nothing but displace the heavenly monarchy onto an earthly monarchy, leaving its power intact."[67] What he is after, instead, is a force of profanation that departs from this dichotomy altogether in order to restore the proper use to a thing that had been wrongly separated from common use. Profanation is accordingly a political act, but one that restores a common usage by not seeking to possess its object. Agamben's methodological aims are thereby disclosed: "Just as the *religio* that is played with but no longer observed opens the gate to use, so the powers of economics, law, and politics, deactivated in play, can become the gateways to a new happiness."[68]

It is perhaps no surprise that Illich's demonstration of the rise of an instrumental rationality that sought to explain the unlimited role of technology at the dawn of modernity also becomes a point of interest to Agamben, who sees such a form of rationality deployed by the Church through its development of a "trinitarian economy and the doctrine of the sacraments."[69] Agamben's critique of these theological foundations, one that runs the entire length of his *Homo Sacer* project, is likewise intended demonstrably to reveal and, in turn, to undermine the political-theological apparatus that has sustained Western subjectivity. In attempting this deconstruction, he again runs close to declaring a form of antinomian thought that, paradoxically, mirrors the critique of a particular strand of Jewish theology offered at one point in history specifically by Pauline Christianity.

This connection linking Illich's project of radical reform to Agamben's "pure antinomianism" that seeks a "form of life" beyond the representations that typically establish what human life is to society has already been noted moreover by John Milbank, whom we saw earlier arguing against Žižek and who takes up both Agamben and Illich within his work *Beyond Secular Order*. In this context, he isolates Illich's work specifically, while also referring to Agamben's critique of Western political order. Milbank's interest in Illich relies upon the latter's claims concerning the corruption of a Christian "divine government through love," turning charity into something that one can order through a bureaucratic efficiency.[70] As Milbank will unfold its basic coordinates,

> If, indeed, Ivan Illich exaggerated in almost seeing schools, hospitals and mad-houses as bad *per se*, surely he did not exaggerate in seeing the

absolutely unprecedented intrusion of the state and the capitalist market into absolutely every aspect of modern human life as a kind of demonic perversion of the "extra" of supernatural charity. According to his thesis, it is not so much that the sense of the supernatural has ever gone away as, rather, that it has been grossly perverted, starting with processes at the heart of Christendom itself, as just detailed. The Christian charitable sense of unlimited inter-involvement and creative capacity to give to the other and so transform it has been mis-deployed as an excuse for the state to pry into and regulate absolutely every aspect of human life—apparently in the interests of our now of course merely animal well-being [...] but really in the concealed interests of the state as an efficiently run machine, and of the extraction from it of the capital of control by those who—for the moment—run it.[71]

Citing Agamben, but really following a thread of Foucault's work within Agamben's writing in many ways, Milbank further comments on how this perversion of Christianity has led to a "disciplinary mode of the pastoral" which then evolved into a "warped anarchic rule of the entirely 'flexible market.'"[72] I find, in general, that Milbank is right to take up this linkage between Illich and Agamben in order to demonstrate a wholescale critique of the disciplinary society much like Taylor had already done.[73] This is, moreover, the site from which we might begin to rethink the role of reform (and hence a sort of "pure antinomianism" or hypernomianism) at the heart of Christian claims, though I am also not convinced that Milbank himself has fully grasped the consequences of Agamben's critique as such.[74] What is exposed through Illich's intervention, however—the radicality that had caused Taylor to waver in his support, but Agamben to find a perhaps kindred spirit—is the role of reform within any given institution, tradition, or structure that needs to be further understood vis-à-vis antinomian, messianic, and even heretical impulses working from within to alter whatever identity appears before us.

The Role of History

Illich, for his part, cites the influence of Gerhart Ladner's *The Idea of Reform* upon his own understanding of institutional critique, a strand of thought that might prove helpful for us to discuss a bit more in-depth in order to illuminate the general dynamics I am seeking to elucidate. For Ladner, there was an irresolvable tension between the subjective impetus for reform (the *idea* of reform, its epistemological or psychological foundation) and the objective, material conditions in which any reform is carried out (its ontological status). It was his opinion, moreover, that only the historian could attempt to suture this fractured state of things (as in Agamben's work, it is only the philosopher who is capable of such suturing).[75] Subjectivity, as such, extends itself through every objective condition and illustrates its steady influence upon the material conditions of reality. Only a form of "historical complementarity," as he would put it, can serve as what brings the subjective and the objective together.[76] What Ladner seems to highlight overall is that which we might see parade under a variety of names and tensions, many of which remain theoretically unresolved—a situation that brings to mind in particular Agamben's admitted call for a "hermeneutical" tension between law and the Church at the same time as he signals for an end to Western apparatuses of subjectivity (and so appears as advocating antinomianism to many observers).[77]

We also see this dynamic, moreover, in such formulations as Erich Fromm's diagnosis of the dialectical tension between disobedience and obedience that characterizes humanity and its history, or Michel de Certeau's contrast between the elite and the masses, which essentially recalls a Marxist reading of that class struggle which underlies all of history itself.[78] What Fromm, for his part, highlights is a prophetic, messianic propensity toward disobedience that frees humanity of an idealized state of nature, subsequently creating its history, but also paradoxically pointing toward the "end of history" wherein such a harmony will be restored.[79] What Fromm grasped in this too was that disobedience, or any deviation from moral norms really, is constituted by our freedom. Or, to put it in Ladner's phrasing, "[…] the idea of reform may now be defined as the idea of free, intentional and ever perfectible, multiple, prolonged and ever repeated efforts by man to reassert and augment values pre-existent in the spiritual-material compound of the world."[80] Reform is, however, as Ladner goes on to caution, "a provisional conceptual tool only," one that "may not always fit the historical material exactly."[81]

If, as for Fromm, our desires for disobedience, but also reform, stem from an idea alone, and not necessarily or solely from our historical conditions, Ladner would seem to agree, though he would also isolate such a dynamic as arising from within the Christian tradition and its ability to abstract itself into philosophical conceptual form apart from the historical and material conditions of "being Jewish." This was to be the Pauline reading of the Christ event that would undo Jewish identity without changing the historical person who either was or was not born Jewish. In fact, such a materialistic identity no longer mattered so long as the "idea" of reform dominated. In Ladner's summation,

> granted the possibility of defining the idea of reform and of studying and describing it as a historical fact, as a phenomenon essentially Christian in origin and early development, it does not follow implicitly that the idea corresponds to a reality. That it often does not is no serious problem, but whether it ever does is a question whereby the terms contained in the definition are transposed from the history of ideology to that of preterideological existence. Is there possibility at least of spirit besides matter, of value besides indifference, of liberty besides determination, of final besides efficient causality, of relative perfectibility besides the absolute, of multiplicity besides unity; in short, is there possibility of reform besides changelessness and besides other types of renewal and change? No cogent answer can be expected from the historical sources alone.[82]

If Ladner is correct in positing historical analysis as the suture, or what provides the complementarity, between the psychological and the material, then we are able to see how the eschatological, viewed as the end of history itself, might actually point us back toward the existence of that which history wrestles with, rather than merely as that which goes *beyond* history. That is, perhaps the end of history is really the domain of the abstract idea *or* the pure material conditions of existence, both of which exist "beyond" history and yet *rely upon* history to make them intelligible in any sense.

Following Adorno, who laid the coordinates for what I am here suggesting, I would argue that any going beyond history (its *transcendence*) is possible only through the fractured immanence before us, a point that Agamben has echoed on numerous occasions as well, and which I have alluded to already. If Judaism could be said to give birth to this relationship between the idea of reform and our lived material conditions (portrayed as the call for justice in terms of one's living material conditions) as what lay at the root of a salvation history, it was Christianity's genius—if I might attempt to put things this way—to simply *repeat* this dynamic relationship itself, devoid of any specific material conditions or context. In the Christian (re)conceptualization of this impetus for reform, even Judaism's particularity is shed so that the idea itself might be further isolated and enacted within history, *as* history, embodied anywhere and potentially by anyone. This is nothing other than the radical impulse that defines any minimal theology and which continuously leaves institutional religious sensibilities in a panic concerning their attempts to defend the particularities of their identities, communities, and traditions.

A Possible Experience of Grace

As but one example of how a radical theology develops in light of these insights, we might now be better able to contemplate the "weak theology" of someone like John Caputo and his unending attempts to reform the Catholic faith by seeming to want to do away with the Church's institutional structure while simultaneously repeating something like the original impetus for the Protestant Reformation. In his estimation, attuning one's ear to the "poetry of Scripture" means to listen to the event happening in the biblical narrative, under it, moving through it, and, in a certain sense too, *beyond* it.[83] In the context of discussing the creation narratives as a "poetic turn" which brings life to a barrenness and not a *creatio ex nihilo*, Caputo tries to define just such religious poetics as "works of religious imagination that give expression to a faith and a hope, a love and a desire, to a religious hermeneutic that the name of God inscribed in things from the start, that the world is marked by the hand of God, that the world bears the stamp of a great and sweeping Yes."[84] Creation comes to express what he terms a "sacred anarchy," or a force which could be called a "poetics of the impossible" that undoes whatever religious representations humanity has worked into shared forms, just as time itself can now be perceived as an endless cycle of creation, destruction, and re-creation.[85] The "Kingdom of God," for Caputo, and here following Derrida rather closely, is the always coming horizon of justice that is never actually historically present to us, that which is regularly interrupted or suspended precisely in order that it might never cease to be caught up in those perpetual asymptotic processes of justice.[86]

Caputo's hope, of course, is that a particular experience of grace might become possible beyond the strict confines of any perceptible sense of normativity, that grace indeed, to paraphrase Pauline thought, might that much more abound. Whether or not such an experience must come about through this dissolution of traditional forms of identity or law is another question, one that is not removed in the least from the center of (post)modern thought. Rather, I would argue, this question lingers in a variety of forms in contemporary thought, none perhaps more emphatically than in the unending theological-historical tension between grace and law.

Whether we call any such attempt to resolve the tension between grace and law the end of the sacred, the genuinely sacred, the force of secularization itself or a profanation beyond any such dichotomous logics, we are faced with the same problematic configuration again and again: How does structure (or law) relate to its reform (as a moment of intrusive grace)? Or, rather, as this debate is often embodied, how does the orthodox relate to the radical?

What I have been gesturing to throughout this brief study so far is an ingenious solution that has been bandied about since the Apostle Paul wrote his letters to the churches, *or even earlier* as it was made manifest within Judaism itself. The only solution worth considering—hence the variety of philosophers and theologians intent on isolating its capacity to dismantle any system without fully doing away with it—is one involving the negation of negation, or the failure of representation, as the only possibility of transcendence. Only here can we find present that which theologically we consider to be a moment of grace through the transcending of law, while at the same time existing as an action that does not eliminate law altogether, hence its *hypernomian* rather than *antinomian* reality. In other words, Taylor's attempt to reframe the division between secularism and religion was not entirely misplaced, as it attempted to reformulate the religious community as one centered on potential "networks of agape" that defy the typical coordinates of communal formation. It was at the same time, however, unable to more fully articulate why the radicality of someone like Illich (or Agamben) is at times necessary to unsettle the dynamics that undergird any human community. What Taylor had only begun to describe was the possibility of access to a form of love, manifest as grace, that exceeds any human relation. This is precisely what I will turn to next in order to further elucidate the contours of what a minimal theology might look like.

3

Grace

The Nihilism of Grace

In the recent philosophical-theological writings of John Caputo, we find a willingness to face the nihilistic threat of living "without purpose" as an ultimately, if paradoxical, hopeful beacon to humanity. In his words,

> [Life] is without a purpose, not because it falls short of a purpose, like an obsolete tool that no longer serves a use, but because it is in excess of a purpose. It is not less than purposeful but more than useful. It is without a purpose in the sense that it cannot be treated as means to some long-term and external end; it does not *serve* a purpose like that. A particular thing in the world may be of service to another, but the world as a whole is not in service. […] But nonetheless it is, as Kant said of the work of art, purposive without having any purpose. It has a strictly internal meaning, its own internal quality, delight, and form, without serving as a means to a further end.[1]

This is the summation of a "purposiveness without purpose" that Caputo has been aiming toward for quite some time in his work and which is a confirmation of the "nihilism of grace" that, he believes, points us toward a form of religious belief beyond that which humanity had previously known or experienced. Removed of its teleological ends, life and faith, like art, appear to be without purpose and yet at the same time they contain an internal purpose of some sort. If there is to be a sense of grace that flows from the establishment of such a position, it is one that comes about only through the reduction of purpose to purposelessness—a movement of apparent "nihilism" that some locate in the concept of inoperativity—but also, in turn, of a movement somehow from purposelessness to another kind of purpose. As Stanley Rosen had once suggested was the real purpose of modern nihilistic views: "Nihilism is fundamentally an attempt to overcome or to repudiate the past on behalf of an unknown and unknowable yet hoped-for future," a sentiment that Derrida, as much as Caputo, might well agree with.[2]

Caputo's pronouncement on life's "purposive purposelessness" formulates itself as well in the manner of a Levinasian (and Derridean) "relation without relation" in that there is an excess of relation that cannot be entirely assimilated *by* the disclosed relation. In other words, there is a sense of "wholly otherness" to that which is related to, and which prevents the relation from entirely foreclosing upon it—its impossibility and what could be considered as a sort of "negative dialectical" relation. Such a grace is to be understood as a "purposefulness without purpose" or "lawfulness without law" that can be said to underwrite an experience that goes "beyond" the ordinary sense of things and cannot be circumscribed by its initial term. Caputo's "nihilism of grace" resonates a good deal, I believe, with my previous comments on antinomianism, but also with Žižek's description of the sublime as an "embodiment of Nothing" that is continuously, and wrongly, given an apparent "body" as it is appropriated by various ideological positions.[3] To refuse to give it a positive "body" would be to accept its nihilistic character and to be transformed by it at the same time. It would be an experience of nothing less than a moment of its peculiar, even paradoxical grace.

For Immanuel Kant, the figure from whom Caputo could be said to truly draw this "purposiveness without purpose," aesthetics is determined by its ability both to appear as lawless in its determination of taste and consequently to exceed its apparent lawlessness in a fashion analogous to a law. This, more than anything else, was what gave art a unique place in human experience, one that extended beyond the boundaries of reason alone and toward something more "fully human." This is the very quality of its extension that would later in the modern period give art the apparent opportunity to replace religion in the modern world. What this juxtaposition of a concept and its negation will add to a conversation on aesthetics is not only a pronouncement on the paradoxical and contradictory nature of art itself but a formulation of the entirely human ability to transcend its own understanding, and thereby as well any explanation for the experience of a certain guilt that lingers in the act of transcendence as one attempts to leave behind the realm of immanence.

We might take, in this regard, not just the attempts to bring the body back into theology (contrary to Bultmann's abstract demythologization, as we saw earlier), but the incomplete though highly suggestive formulation of aesthetics in the work of Adorno, for whom every "work of art has its irresoluble contradiction in the 'purposefulness without purpose' by which Kant defined the aesthetic."[4] For Adorno, the contradiction that sustains all art is bound up with art's artificiality, a matter of being a "second creation" that "postulates itself as absolute, purpose-free, existing in itself," at once caught up with a sense of "rational purposefulness" at the same moment as it tries to free itself from such a state in a flourish of inherent lawlessness.[5] In this contradictory movement, the social function of art *is* its functionlessness.[6] Art is consequently defined in terms of its capacity for a creative use of negativity that Adorno would trace much further than its more limited usage in the realm of aesthetics, and, as we have already seen, into the domain of all conceptualization.

Rather than simply hold that such a negative gesture is entirely beneficial, however, Adorno considers the dynamic internal to the creation of all "artifact" (artifice, artificiality) as it introduces a "false consciousness" to the production of art—its "fetish character," he will say—that induces a sense of guilt within the individual who produces the artwork in the first place. Though this may seem like the death-knell to the human desire to create art (or concepts, even language itself), it is rather the case that, in his words, "[...] the guilt of fetishism does not disqualify art, any more so than it disqualifies anything culpable; for in the universally, socially mediated world nothing stands external to its nexus of guilt. The truth content of artworks, which is indeed their social truth, is predicated on their fetish character."[7] To be human is to deal relentlessly in artifice and artifact. To be human is to create that which introduces purpose through its very purposelessness and which identifies the guilt that humanity is enmeshed within, forever separated from any illusory state of nature (or grace) beyond such guilt. There is simply no way to overcome such a "nexus of guilt" bound up with the separation of the spiritual and the material (or, likewise, the "natural" and the "artificial"), which the presence of the artwork—or our very desire for the artwork to come to life even—brings prominently to light.[8]

Art is, at its most primordial level, inextricably intertwined with the desire to break free of the natural and to produce an artificial representation of nature, to construct a contradictory artificiality that subsists in the form of a purposive purposelessness. It is only by embracing such a fetishistic, contradictory existence that art has the potential to create another path by which to walk through the "natural" world around us and to provide a type of liberation— that is, to envision alternative political and social imaginations. This is where art confronts a non-ideological paradoxical existence. This task, I would add, is precisely what Illich had been gesturing toward in his formulations of a radical Christianity beyond any institutional relationship.

The Entrance of the Sublime

The question upon which these reflections are centered essentially concerns the existence and nature of a "free lawfulness" that registers a paradox or contradiction in its very existence, but which also attempts to serve as mediator between the inherent lawfulness of understanding and the free play of the imagination. The "peculiarity of a judgment of taste," alongside the "free lawfulness of the understanding," to put things in their Kantian context, arises from the attempt of the imagination to conceptualize according to the laws of understanding, but yet without necessarily an objective "correspondence" to reality. The imagination, by its nature, must be able to push beyond observable (objective) reality in order to formulate its (subjective) correspondence to the imagination of the individual alone.[9] This process will entail the apparent "failure" of the imagination in that it is not able to reach beyond the limits of reason in terms of what it can articulate intelligibly, even as it strives to do precisely that, and even finds some pleasure in going beyond the limits of what had appeared to contain it.

What we encounter in this permanent inbuilt tension between understanding (formed through the bonds of established procedures and norms) and imagination (as a utopian desire to reshape those very procedures and norms) is a situation wherein, as Eli Friedlander has described it, the mind appears to negatively present "its own incomparable immeasurability."[10] The experience of the sublime will not simply present us with a feeling of that which is entirely external to us; it will present to us the reality of not only our own minds, and so too their limits, *but also* our ability to somehow go beyond them, to evidence what Freidlander calls the "uncanniness" of our "condition" as human beings.[11] The Freudian and even pseudo-religious usage of the term "uncanny" at this point would seem entirely appropriate as well, since our experience of such a state will appear to us as at once part of us while also entirely being beyond us at the same time. The tensions that have characterized the competition between the orthodox and the radical would also seem to overlap neatly upon this configuration of aesthetic relations.

In contrast to the beautiful which presents us with a type of positive content, the sublime functions negatively, refusing to present us with any content per se, only skirting the limits and conditions of sensibility, and making our ability to coordinate judgments based upon an experience of the sublime a terribly difficult and highly subjective thing to do.[12] From this state of experience arise the individualistic preferences of aesthetic taste, which, I would posit, function somewhat analogously to the formation of one's conscience in certain theological traditions. In John Henry Newman's rendering, for example, the conscience is certainly a subjective construct, one that we must adhere to even when we appear to be standing against the traditions or doctrines of authority. Nevertheless, it is the conscience too that is shaped in the individual *through* those very same traditions and doctrines (as well as experiences, reasons, opinions, prejudices, and so forth) that it may also stand against. The *sensus communis* that circumscribes the formation of conscience and the manner by which it judges moral action would seem then to function in a significant, parallel manner to aesthetic, and even political, judgment.

For Kant, the lawless play of the imagination results in a kind of "lawfulness without law" or a "purposiveness without an end."[13] The free play of the imagination means that "stiff regularity" spells the limits of what satisfies the imaginative and creative acts that humanity "makes happen."[14] Appearing at times as wholly beyond our rational capacities, but also in such a way as to confirm their entirely human nature, the drive to create art and to experience the sublime beyond the limits of our understanding puts us in a sort of ecstatic state of being, one that is rightly described by that paradoxical and contradictory modern label of the fetishistic. Much as with the creation of the fetish that denies any direct answer to the question of whose hands created the (artificial) object—the divine or the human?—genius in art becomes for Kant that which functions in such a way as to not understand itself or its own capacities. It becomes an innate quality through which nature grants "the rule to art."[15]

Indeed, the manner through which the aesthetic mediates between nature and art becomes the basis for the expression of human freedom itself, and despite, as Adorno had noted, any guilt that accrues naturally throughout the process.[16] The freedom that we access through art and our reflections upon it runs necessarily counter to the exercise of power, or that which is typically justified through recourse to nature—hence art's transformative political and social capacity.[17] The faculty of taste is consequently involved not so much with apprehending that which it deems beautiful but in the invention of and resonance with one's fantasies, as Kant puts it.[18] In the end, the "abstraction from all constraint by rules" becomes the means by which "taste can demonstrate its greatest perfection in projects of the imagination."[19] In this way, taste functions as an a-historical, individualized measure in relation to the imagination, though it is also historical insofar as it too must rely upon the *sensus communis* in order to determine its shape. This is a tension that will not go away and will not be easy to theorize as a singular, cohesive activity of judgment. Indeed, the realm of aesthetics is one that contains a permanent split between beauty and the sublime that cannot simply be sutured together, but which cannot be sundered either. This tension clearly parallels that between the community and the radical, negative critiques that constantly appear concerning it.

What I want to note at this point is the significant insight which this analysis yields for the parallel tensions between the orthodox and the radical, whose use of poetry (and any accompanying theo-poetics) often defines those in search of a minimal theological point of view. The tension between the beautiful, defined through a shared, communal experience, and the sublime, which breaks the intelligibility of the beautiful in order to expand our experience of aesthetics, is played out in political terms by the institutionalized orthodox, who typically define what is considered as beautiful in a given context, and the radicals, who imagine another world in order to break through whatever established coordinates define a given cultural sensibility.

The experience of beauty in particular is predicated upon the apprehension of form, and the sublime that of its formlessness, but also its sense of limitlessness that is yet, paradoxically, somehow represented as a "totality."[20] Beauty is concerned with quality, the sublime with quantity. The beautiful feels as if it promotes life through the pleasure it induces, whereas the sublime seems only indirectly to bring itself about through "a momentary inhibition of the vital powers and the immediately following and all the powerful outpouring of them."[21] The sublime, though it is "absolutely great" and so beyond all forms of comparison, evokes also a "negative pleasure" in that it brings about as much repulsion as attraction, leading one to respect or admire it, though not necessarily to derive pleasure from the experience of it. That which brings about a feeling of the sublime in us is rather "[...] contrapurposive for our power of judgment, unsuitable for our faculty of presentation, and as it were doing violence to our imagination, but is nevertheless judged all the more sublime for that."[22]

The sublime, much in accord with what I have already described, represents a paradox in that what is absolutely (infinitely) great is nonetheless sought through comprehension in terms of the concepts to which it tries to subordinate the infinite.[23] A sense of negative pleasure comes about as we sense the "feeling of displeasure from the inadequacy of the imagination" in aesthetic matters, while also experiencing a certain pleasure in going beyond where reason had failed.[24] There is thus no "calm," as Kant puts it, as would ordinarily surround the contemplation of the beautiful. The sublime instead moves us through an experience of the tensions that permanently displace our capacity for inscribing the (in)describable within reason. The individual experience of the sublime highlights our failure to present that which exceeds all imaginative representation.[25] In many ways, and building off of the preceding analysis, the sublime would seem to be *the* experience of the hypernomian desire to go beyond the staid, comfortable norms of representation that are shared by a community. As Jean-François Lyotard would himself interpret the sublime: it is what allows the unpresentable to become presentable, or, in other words, to think representation beyond all known forms of representation.[26] In this way, the sublime, as a subjective experience beyond shared forms of representation, maintains a political dimension focused on the absolute singularity of an individual subjectivity.[27]

The sublime, Kant stresses, cannot be felt through fear, but only through that which "elevates the strength of our soul above its usual level" insofar as we are able to "discover within ourselves a capacity for resistance of quite another kind, which gives us the courage to measure ourselves against the apparent all-powerfulness of nature."[28] In other words, the sublime confronts us with our "physical powerlessness," but also with the sense that we stand somewhat apart from it, capable of cultivating a sense of "superiority over nature." A "power" within us that is *not* of our nature, but is rather our truest "vocation," arises internally and offers us the chance to find pleasure (through safety) in what is displeasing (the sensation of fear). For this reason, Kant will conclude, the general in the field of war is considered closer to accessing the sublime than the politician who remains at a distance from that which is immediately feared.[29] There is in this formulation of things a sense that one's vocation flows not from our nature, but from that which exceeds us—another point of opening toward the potentially religious domain from within the experience of the sublime, but in such a way as to radically challenge whatever configuration of the religious had been constructed. There is a sense that the sublime might grant us access to the nature both of sovereignty and of powerlessness at the same time—indeed as they may even arise from a shared location. What the sublime offers is the poverty of any given (sovereign) religion insofar as the sublime represents not only the deconstruction of an established, historical institution, identity, or tradition but also the traces of a minimal theology within a given religious definition of the sacred.

Accessing the Possibility of Grace

The sublime, as it occurs in nature, is certainly formless, but nonetheless capable of being an "object of pure satisfaction," evidencing as such its ability to "demonstrate subjective purposiveness" in some measure, though exactly how it functions as an *a priori* subjective principle remains the question that Kant intended to sort out as central to the conditions of a (again, subjective) critique of taste, especially since the establishment of such an *a priori* lies at the base of all transcendental philosophy.[30] The problematic deepens, of course, when the *a priori* condition that is sought after is not one that takes place on the objective level, but on the subjective—*the* site from which aesthetic judgment arises in the first place. What turns out to be the "subjective condition of all judgments" is in fact the faculty or power of judgment itself and a return to the objective and universal.[31] In many ways, again, this tension echoes that between the religious community as the governor of beauty and the secular individual as a site of sublime subjectivity.

The freedom that the imagination utilizes—that is, one lacking any purely conceptual basis—dictates that the faculty of judgment rest upon a permanent tension between the imagination and understanding, or freedom and lawfulness. The feeling that arises within the person performing such a judgment is one that is based on "the purposiveness of the representation" so that we might have an intelligible understanding of the object being judged.[32] In this play of activities and faculties, the difference between aesthetic judgments and theoretical ones is that the former is both the object and the law that judges it—what seems to define the realm of the subjective—whereas the latter involves the categorizing of judgments beneath objective concepts that construct the foundations of our understanding.[33] This inward turn toward the "indeterminate" conceptualizations that characterize the subjective is the only possible resolution of the antinomy, or paradox, that defines aesthetic judgment: its appearing to be both based and not based on a conceptual (law-like) approach.[34] In Kant's words, "The subjective principle, namely the indeterminate idea of the supersensible in us, can only be indicated as the sole key to demystifying this faculty which is hidden to us even in its sources, but there is nothing by which it can be made more comprehensible."[35]

Since the supersensible can only remain indeterminate, however, the most we can infer from its existence, and we are guided in doing so by the imperative that we must make reason "self-consistent,"[36] is that there must be a teleological end toward which this indeterminateness is directed. This is where Kant will conclude his third *Critique*, though it is also the juncture at which he is able to point directly toward how such an inference of a teleological end might lead us toward another way to prove the existence of God—that which he takes up in an appendix and which is entirely consistent with his prioritization of reason's inaccessibility to the divine. What will unfold from this, and though Kant had not entirely foreseen it coming, is that in the absence of a *teleological* purpose which he will effectively remove, and as would later be found in the works of both Schopenhauer and Nietzsche, there is only the human "will," with no divinity left in sight.[37]

In practical terms, the problem of how we are to rely upon a subjective *a priori* is resolved when Kant looks toward the *sensus communis* as what precedes the power of judgment, that is, an historical and evolving tradition of "common sense" that lies at the base not only of all aesthetic judgment but of legal judgment as well.[38] In such a way, the *sensus communis* functions much like a *fidei depositum* or the "deposit of faith" from which any governing tradition flows.[39] Such an overlap between the foundations of religious doctrine and aesthetic judgment, when both are perceived in their historical, traditional forms, is not the only major theological implication that will arise from within a consideration of Kant's paradoxical formulations of the "purposive purposelessness." The sublime, insofar as it appears as a gratuitous gift of nature that points toward its limitations, but also as it goes beyond them, is, as Friedlander puts it, a moment of grace in the life of the human being.[40] Or, in the words of Caputo, "Purposelessness is not a problem but the very condition of grace, of the gift of grace, which comes without benefactor or debt."[41] To be shown the limits of our nature and to confront its purposelessness, but also to experience in the sublime encounter a life capable of being lived beyond what we had thought those limits to be (even if experienced purely as an internal phenomenon, and as *the* sought-after goal of the form of life in the works of both Foucault and Agamben), and thereby to find purpose and meaning through such an encounter *are* the fundamental essence of grace.

It is this dynamic that ensures that the orthodox believer needs the radical imagination to intrude and upend its most cherished, even beautiful, representations. It is the radicality of the sublime moment of grace that allows the orthodox position to have something like an experience of grace at all. This is the experience of grace as an exception to the normal state of affairs that many, including Carl Schmitt, had understood to be the foundations of sovereign power, but which, I have contended throughout, are not to be taken as such. Rather, such an experience of sublime grace is a kenotic pouring out that can only offer humanity a minimal theology *at most*.

In this moment of the experience of grace, encountered within the crises of reason and representation, we find a new form of sovereignty wholly unlike one rooted in our alleged "origins," the outcome of a negative dialectics that Adorno himself had perhaps failed to fully realize. We can locate in this movement a possible form of sublime grace founded upon what Christoph Menke has described as an aesthetic negativity that maintains a manner of sovereignty precisely through its ability to bring about a crisis at the heart of reason.[42] The sense of autonomy that aesthetics brings about for the individual is predicated upon its ability to foment a moment of crisis within an otherwise monolithic state of being. Autonomy, then, is almost paradoxically guaranteed in the same instance as one's assumed sense of self falls apart, giving rise to—and here once again attaining something like the register of the religious language that the entrance of grace calls us to be particularly attentive to—potential moments of personal transformation and inner conversion.

The Restoration of Tradition

The question of tradition, alongside that of grace, is a major principle that remains somewhat under-theorized in all of this speculative discourse on the aesthetic, the limits of human understanding, and the sublime or religious encounter. I invoke the term "tradition" here not in a Gadamerian sense, as that which corresponds to an unending process involving the "fusion of horizons" as a hermeneutical act that seemingly pivots wholly on the perception of the beautiful and as an asymptotic approach to understanding in general, but rather as a hermeneutical principle that involves the interruption of understanding by the sublime as the sublime is potentially brought before our consciousness *by* tradition—if such a thing is even to be considered as possible.[43] As Kirk Pillow has already effectively argued, our use of the sublime as what deconstructs our normal, rational patterns might be what actually enables us to construct a variety of networks for understanding one another that are based on the situations in which we find ourselves, not then on an abstracted, universal, and purely conceptual basis, but rather on whatever empirical and contextual grounds we find ourselves.[44] If such a thing as an authentically human tradition arises from these networked formulations based on a fundamentally sublime disruption of reason (parallel to Taylor's Christian "networks of agape," as we saw earlier), then it functions in a manner profoundly unlike typical instances and uses of tradition. Asking questions about tradition in this context, however, might just allow us to return to other concrete political forms, such as history, institutions, and particular political formations, from a perspective that accounts for both the defenders of communal understanding (the orthodox) and those who would challenge its often hegemonic hold (the radicals).

If the sublime upends a community's sense of the beautiful, while also demonstrating their inseparable bond, I want to ask whether and to what degree tradition can be responsible for maintaining our willingness to encounter the sublime as a reminder and corrective to any complacency we have stagnated in as a result of our search for the beautiful. In deconstructivist language, tradition can only be attentive to its own internal messianic forces which do not in themselves constitute an institution or tradition, but which remain active within any given tradition, though they function analogously to the sublime in a certain sense. Derrida, again, despite being often mistaken as advocating a contrary position, was steadfast in his belief that we must maintain canonical forms and institutions which were only capable of being deconstructed and reconstructed again insofar as they existed in the first place—a concession to a process far more hermeneutical than has generally been recognized (and perhaps akin to Paul Ricoeur's threefold process of totalization, de-totalization, and re-totalization that so frequently permeated his own work).

To focus the question still further: Is there a form of messianic (or apophatic or even nihilistic) grace operative within our encounter with the sublime that tradition would have to safeguard and promote, even at the cost of weakening its own structures (its "strength") within the social world that gave birth to them? To explicitly invoke a theological register, could this be what characterizes the Church (as "networks of agape") or the Kingdom of God above all else, a willingness to weaken itself, to take on a form of existence through a welcomed embrace of its own inclination toward a state of poverty?

There is no doubt that the question of tradition is one that undercuts many constructed forms of subjectivity, especially those that trigger theological considerations from a Pauline perspective: the many returns to Saint Paul today that seek to derive from his thought a sort of militant universal subject, from Jacob Taubes to Alain Badiou and from Slavoj Žižek to Giorgio Agamben.[45] It would seem that Paul was eager to establish a form of subjectivity that was *not* subject to the "powers of this world," one that would render all social and political representations of personal and collective identity as internally void (or negated). As I have noted already, each socially intelligible identity was divided by Paul from within so that there was no longer male nor female, slave nor free, Jew nor Greek (Galatians 3:28), but only the servant of Christ who died with Christ, no longer alive to the representations that society imposes upon individuals, but alive to the figure of Christ who moves beyond what appears to have its being. The division of flesh and spirit within a social representation saw to the *internal* division of a *social* division (identity) that would be cancelled, in a sense, but also still perceived as socially or religiously intelligible.

The quality of living "as if not" ascribed to a particular identity—for example, living "as if not" married for the sake of the coming Kingdom of God, in Paul's parlance—was a hallmark of his radical thought and a major reason that he was able to seemingly endorse various status quo positions in that he was radically undermining their descriptive force (see 1 Corinthians 7). We might think in this regard of his advice to the runaway slave Onesimus that he should return to his master because his identity as a slave was rendered null and void by his "death in Christ." He was "no longer as a slave, but more than a slave" (Philemon 16), which prompted Paul to encourage a return to his master since he was, spiritually, not subject to anyone, but, physically "in the flesh," still subject to political laws, institutions, social collectives, and the like. What such a reading of the radical subjectivity that accompanies the follower of Christ entails ends up being characterized by a fundamental ambivalence toward historical forms, a perception that became painfully obvious in his wavering between an expectation of the coming of Christ that was at times immanent and at other times deferred (e.g., 1 Corinthians 7:29). This insight might go some ways as well toward explaining the fact that Paul appeared to have no interest in the historical person of Jesus.

What each of the contemporary philosophical accounts of Pauline subjectivity lacks is precisely a hermeneutical explanation of how the Pauline subject of universality is supposed to stand vis-à-vis tradition, and specifically the historically unjust structures that are often maintained within a given tradition. The inability to theorize such an expansive hermeneutic lies not only at the base of the problematic that haunts biblical interpretation (e.g., how slavery was later abolished despite biblical justification for its institution being quite pronounced) but also deep within those recoveries of Pauline thought that fail to theorize how tradition can also be said to stand in permanent tension with its own messianic forces.

It is no surprise that an explicit engagement with the dynamics of tradition is generally lacking in these accounts, which are forced to justify a form of subjectivity that transcends any socially intelligible matrix of representations, but which is nonetheless unable to determine just how we are to work within a given tradition or political context. Though it may sound somewhat like a facile critique of their political views on tradition, to suggest that Derrida and Agamben have struggled to articulate a reasonable relationship to tradition is not a stretch of the imagination—it is rather characteristic of defending a form of (Pauline) subjectivity shorn of a hermeneutic involving history. It is also why those who follow in their path, as with John Caputo, for instance, are often convinced of the need to have a particular, historical religious tradition in one's establishment of their identity, though which religion in particular does not really matter.

This tension between historical tradition and a universal subject who exceeds the boundaries of history is manifest in a productive sense in the work of Judith Butler, among others, who has recognized the necessity to deconstruct certain "unjust" social representations while also respecting the manner in which a politically and culturally acknowledged legitimation of individual subjectivity does actually contain a psychological benefit that is necessary for life to flourish and for those living on the margins of society. Only in such a way, she claims, can certain excluded persons come to feel not only accepted but also "alive" in a sense (i.e., legally and socially recognized).[46] In acknowledging this tension, there is an inherent hermeneutical respect for the balance between maintaining traditional structures and undoing them that cannot be neglected or dismissed.

The difficulty with presenting tradition as a necessary vehicle for preserving one's encounter with the sublime that undoes it, however, is that tradition can also be an ideological container for what appears as sublime, but which is more or less a fetishistic temptation to replace the "nothingness" of the sublime with a promised positive content—the "sublime object of ideology," as Žižek has put it, and which certainly resonates with one version of the theological paradoxes that has historically fostered political obedience, as noted in the first chapter.[47] In Adorno's phrasing of things, "It is nothing new to find that the sublime becomes the cover for something low."[48] And so we must ask, again and again, as a safeguard against positing such a "sublime object of ideology," how we are to encounter the sublime (or paradox, as discussed in the first chapter) without necessarily or immediately giving it a positive content, but rather to let it subject our subjectivities, so to speak, to their undoing—a negative eschatological project that would rather incline us toward embracing the poverty of our being rather than seek to re-establish some form of sovereign power in the face of an unyielding "nothingness"?[49] Again, however, this does not preclude any identity or tradition from eventually taking shape; it rather opens up the space for self-reflexive, critical thought to appear in much-needed, and at times oppressive or (repressively) violent, contexts.

The Aesthetic Solution

Terry Eagleton, for one, has described the modern foundations of culture in relation to the "death of God" in a way that resonates deeply with definitions of the aesthetic as well as the ideological implications that follow from its use that I have been outlining thus far. As the "supplement or prosthesis" to reason, as he calls it, the aesthetic, in order to legitimate sovereign rule, attempts to connect the "lived experience" of ordinary people to their understanding of life (its "enlightened" and superior abstraction), something accomplished through ordinary experiences of beauty. This performance of the aesthetic is maintained so that a governing power might become, as he puts it, "ideologically effective."[50] Experiences of the beautiful within society, presumably from fashion to decoration to film and multiple mediums of art in general, can be utilized as a means of pacifying individuals—or, in Kantian terms, "calming" their souls.

For the most part, Kant's notion of aesthetic judgment had functioned as a mediating reality between the subjective and the objective, "personal assent" and "universal agreement" in Eagleton's rephrasing.[51] Aesthetics became the conditioning grounds for belief as it arose somewhere between feeling and thought. If religion had previously been able to arouse belief within a similar juncture, it was here supplanted by the aesthetic, though it remained unclear to many whether such beliefs were formed in explicit relationship to the beautiful or to the sublime. Either way, they were formed as a sort of "taste" or "preference" that presented itself as a livable truth, raising interesting questions along the way about the formations of truth and belief as they relate to the *sensus communis* and individual aesthetic experience. In many ways, Kant's descriptions of aesthetic judgment, as it forms something like a space for belief within the individual, foreshadow later developments in understanding the complex calculus that determines one's faith (somewhat akin to John Henry Newman's sense of the probabilities that actually give rise to faith).

God, however, in Kant's (re)fashioning of things, had been relocated to "the trackless spaces of the sublime," from which we might eventually be able to deduce God's potential existence, but which at the same time also places God far beyond any human understanding. As such, God was pitched at a remove from human affairs and even perceived as unable to govern in any effective sense, leaving both the experience of the beautiful and the power of the sovereign on this side of human understanding and in what is considered to be the domain of the practical.[52] This isolation or alienation of the divine within the realm of the sublime offers us another pathway from which to view the critique and concomitant distancing of religion from the everyday practical affairs and legitimations of human activity, which would be more helpfully rooted in experiences of beauty. At the same time, however, it also threatens to remove the experience of the sublime as a necessary corrective to human isolation, and as a possible path toward revitalizing something like the genuinely "religious" within ordinary human life.

Art and religion rival each other in the sense that both seek to generate meaning in the modern world, though religion has been more ideologically effective precisely where reason and its (aesthetic) culture have failed to connect to the lives and experiences of ordinary people.[53] Aesthetic signs, much as Schmitt had viewed political ones, are "displaced fragments of theology."[54] Previously, forms of pre-modern religion, which included all senses of the aesthetic within it, had been so successful on the level of everyday life because they were able to assist the individual in ascertaining their identity through the relationship between freedom, autonomy, and self-determination *and* our "dependency on language and culture," a precarious relationship that Eagleton defines as a grace given to humanity.[55]

What Kant's theory on aesthetic judgment ultimately reveals to us, and as we have already noted, is a massive gulf between reason and imagination, as well as between the beautiful and the sublime. This is a split that forces normal perceptions into the dichotomous representations of a sublime-free aesthetic experience of beauty and a religiously sublime experience beyond a shared articulation of it. The former would seem to offer humanity an everyday sense of something akin to the religious, but it would also, Eagleton concludes, fail to actually provide what the religious had once been able to. From the other side of things, the sublime would still contain the possibility of upending our complacency and calm, but it has been pushed to the fringes of language, and so mired in an imaginative realm that, for most, seemed wholly unintelligible and so essentially removed from everyday experience—and with no tradition to preserve its traces (what many today might consider to be the *spiritual* domain entirely removed from having to be *religious* in any concrete sense). In a certain fashion, secularism would appear in these terms as not necessarily a removal of the divine from our world, but as a distancing of the sublime experience that might lead to an encounter with *something like the divine*, though beyond the traditional realm of religious paradoxes that had been used to justify sovereign forms of power. It is this political valence of secularism that is often overlooked by those more concerned with wielding religious power than in analyzing *their own relationship* to power.

Yet, we might ask, what will come to supplant the tension between reason and the aesthetic experience of the sublime? If one continues to need the other, but has great difficulty in doing so, is there anything that can guarantee our taking seriously the inherent and necessary tension between them in such a way as to preserve beauty, reason, and understanding alongside the sublime, the imagination, and religious experience? Can the orthodox be convinced that the radicals are not just helpful at times to upend one's complacency, but necessary to the life of a tradition?

Eagleton, much as I am here also advocating, interestingly turns toward the historical existence of tradition(s) as a possible means of preserving the necessity for such tensions, looking at their "organic" development to be that which lasts after all other models and solutions are examined and found wanting. The mere existence of a tradition—the *sensus communis* again—however, does not placate all our concerns. For example, would such an endorsement of tradition, as Eagleton points out, merely replicate the status quo and undermine any genuine revolutionary change?[56] As he puts it, the organic growth of a tradition as a legitimating foundation can itself serve as a mystification of the real fundaments of power—a point that captures the essence of (Protestant) Reformation thought.[57] Or is the imagination to serve, as it has already on so many occasions, as a means by which grace enters our world for those very few persons who are capable of grasping its aesthetic "truth"—the other Protestant (Calvinistic) and somewhat elitist temptation that undergirds such reform-minded efforts?[58] The question that is being asked in many ways—one akin to the musings that Taylor gave us earlier—is simply whether or not tradition can suture together these divided perspectives, offering us a chance to bring together viewpoints often kept at a great distance across a wide gulf, while subsequently also offering us an opportunity to bring religion back into a broader social and political conversation. Will our use of tradition allow access to the sublime and thus be a helpful corrective to the numbing comfort of beauty? Or will we become complacent precisely through the use of tradition so that we fail to invoke the sublime encounter altogether?

For his part, Eagleton seems to want to recover what is best in Kant's aesthetics concerning the sublime experience while also challenging it through the experiences of tradition and community. Kant, he adds, seems to have missed the opportunity to critically evaluate tradition altogether, leaving religious tradition in particular entirely at a remove from these dynamics. Eagleton suggests that by doing so Kant missed an occasion to perceive the sublime object within the tortured body of "a reviled political criminal," one who is only capable of being part of "divine sovereignty" insofar as this is to be understood as a critique of all human sovereign power, not a condoning of it—a somewhat Barthian proposition.[59] It is in this sense that the gap between beauty and the sublime, as between reason and imagination, offers a sort of permanent critique of all human affairs and keeps the divine at an (apparently) appropriate distance from humanity. As Eagleton reminds us, and in such a way as to point toward the significance of Christianity in particular as a possible way of bridging the gaps that Kant exposed,

> It is graven images, not human ones, that the Mosaic Law forbids, setting its face against idolatry and reification. If there can be no humanly

fashioned icons of Yahweh, it is because the only authentic image of him is humanity itself, and one human individual in particular. Sensible images of the ineffable are generally known as symbols, another shamefaced piece of theology. The model of how a lowly piece of matter comes to smack of the infinite is how the parcel of flesh known as Jesus is the incarnate Son of God.[60]

The gap, as Kant had also pointed out, is one between the infinite and the finite, the irreconcilable division that the figure of Christ had intended to overcome through the Incarnation—one of the traditional theological paradoxes, as I noted in the first chapter. The Christian imagination, then, in a very specific sense serves as an "anti-aesthetic" creed, one that at times elevates the sublime over the beautiful, and offers humanity a chance to reconcile the base division within itself between these competing forces, as between reason and imagination.[61] But this is not the last word from a theological point of view of course. Eagleton's critique of Kant runs parallel not only to the Barthian embrace of Kierkegaard as already noted but to two other ones that I would like to highlight, that of Charles Taylor and of Hans Urs von Balthasar.

In Taylor's reading of the rise of the "secular age," the sublime that exists outside of us eventually comes to provide the basis for an establishment of the sublime within us—the sublimity of reason itself, or the human being—that which both Schopenhauer and Nietzsche praised as the wilder nature of humankind.[62] The modern "buffered" self, as Taylor suggests, stands at a certain remove from the abyss of nature and so is capable, while confronting the sublime within nature, of experiencing something like an "awakening" to "an awareness of ourselves as noumenal beings, who stand as high above all this merely sensible reality, as within the sensible realm the threatening reality stands above our puny phenomenal selves."[63] We are capable of experiencing, through our encounter with the sublime in nature, the moral law within us, as when Kant beheld this practical moral law's sublimity as being on par with the "starry heavens above."⁶⁴ Religion is, in this way, relegated to within the limits of such a moral law founded upon reason itself. Taylor is rightly critical of such an easy reduction of the infinite to its place within the finite, and on much the same grounds that von Balthasar likewise contests this Kantian gesture.

For the Catholic theologian Hans Urs von Balthasar, moral sublimity is substituted for God's glory.⁶⁵ In short, "[…] it is the inner *sublimity* of reason which, despite all its finitude, has penetrated to the Infinite, which reveals God to it, and not for instance God's own sublime glory, which reason in its pure form cannot perceive."⁶⁶ As Taylor has observed, reason becomes its own measure and serves as a reminder of the inaccessibility of "God's own sublime glory," a move which in and of itself ranks Kant, for von Balthasar, up there among the great negative theologians of history, albeit one who removes empirical experience from the transcendental method.⁶⁷ On his own account, von Balthasar merely points out how Kant himself drew a firm line between the sublime foundations of the moral law within us, the very thing that gives rise to a concept of duty through its existing as an "unconditional necessity," and grace, which offers us something more contingent and which we are under no duty to provide. What is determined as sublime has no access to grace, and operates as if radically deviant from such grace in a certain sense.

When von Balthasar turns to consider the nature of the beautiful as a "form of purposiveness" yet without purpose, he avers that such a state destroys any relationship between the beautiful and the true and the good, hence coming to possess meaning only in itself. Hence he provides an abstraction that gives rise to his consideration of Kant as "the first theoretician of *abstract art*."⁶⁸ His conclusion is therefore stark:

[beauty …] possesses exactly the same indefinite character of the finite in itself which, when the rigour of the ethical imperative wants and is no longer seen, can at some point lead to the pure play of finite existence in nothingness with itself, a play which is not only disinterested and without purpose (*l'art pour l'art*) but also ultimately lacking in meaning.[69]

The sublime within the human being replaces the glory or majesty of God, and beauty is sundered from truth and goodness, leaving it bereft of all intelligible meaning. In such comments, we can sense not only von Balthasar's caution concerning Kantian aesthetics but also, I would argue, Taylor's repeated hesitations concerning a postmodern, Nietzschean sensibility—one that culminates in an apparent, ceaseless Derridean sense of play, where meaning can never be fixed once and for all.[70] What we are left to conclude is that equating the true with the beautiful and the good would presumably override such permanent play.

What Eagleton, Taylor, and von Balthasar help us to see, and again in line with certain notions of paradox that miss the possibility of *another* existing form of paradox, are the significant limitations imposed upon religion when the sublime experience is taken to replace the "glory" of the infinite in its own right. It is easy to see, from this perspective, why certain theological imperatives to maintain an absolute gap between humanity and the divine—what Gary Dorrien is right to call the "Barthian revolt" in modern theology[71]—have had such success in appealing to the general Christian landscape in the West.[72] They also, however, keep alive the quest for a sovereign power made operative through paradox and which brings their entire projects under intense political scrutiny at times. The question that remains for us at this point therefore is: But what kind of a glory are we talking about when it is suggested, as von Balthasar does, that the glory of the Lord is what we are after? How are we not, following Agamben's sustained critique of the concept of glory in ancient and modern theo-political contexts, simply reprising an entirely immanent, political idea of glory that is superimposed upon a divine being by a humanity that frequently wishes to grant it an undefinable power?[73] As history well teaches us, this has been all-too-often the political temptation of the orthodox.

Perhaps, however, there is another way to read Kant, one that both recognizes the strand of critique that I have been following thus far and points toward the fracture within Kant's work as also being the source of its reconciliation with the theological after all. That is, what Eagleton seems to isolate that both Taylor and von Balthasar do not highlight in their accounts, at least, is that perhaps rather than simply discarding Kant's account of the beautiful, what if there was a way to encounter the sublime, or glory, or *both*, from within the fracturing of the beautiful itself—in its poverty as it were? Perhaps this would be the way to return to the tautological grounding of sovereign power, of narrative and identity, but from another perspective altogether. It would also demonstrate, once again, the power of a double negation or negative dialectics within philosophical and theological thought.

The Poverty of Grace

Theologically, the concept of grace has always been introduced through the freedom one experiences (in Christ) in relation to, and so somehow never fully apart from, the (Mosaic) Law. It is a grace that is, in a most notorious phrasing of things, a *fulfillment* of the Law (Matthew 5:17). That is, it becomes an imaginative reworking of the Law that at once suspends its rule while also adhering more closely to it than the Law itself would be capable of realizing. I would suggest, in Pauline terms, that the experience of grace that is the Law's fulfillment is a negation of the Law's original negation, in the sense that the Law (not just religious, but all law actually) serves to reduce (or negate) the fullness of the human person for the purposes of legal, cultural, social, political, or religious representation. Under the Law's initial act of negation, we are no longer an indescribable essence or fullness of human potential (a potential form of life); we are rather, man or woman, the citizen of a particular nation-state, a murderer, tax offender, refugee, stateless person, and so forth. Grace functions, in this sense, as that which does not do away with such divisions—this is the hastily formed supercessionist mistake—but instead negates the legal distinction altogether, dividing it further from within.

Though Caputo's "nihilism of grace" may sound overly reductionistic of the human person, and potentially antinomian to some ears, there is no doubt that the emptying out of the human person does precede any reception of grace, a process that might be more accurately characterized as one involved with the "poverty of spirit." It is in this sense alone that something like the beautiful might possibly be apprehended—only after the sublime experience has emptied us through its grace. God's grace, as the political theologian Johann Baptist Metz has described it, is an "intensification" and "outdoing" of our human poverty, one that finds its perfection in God's pouring out of God's own self (*kenosis*) in order to take on the form of a human in utter powerlessness. This is not only an exemplification of the poverty of God—what might otherwise appear to us as the *nihilism of God*—but it is also an act pointing toward a more proper understanding of the potentiality of the human being, one only embraced through a redoubled intensification of human poverty, not its absolute eradication. In this too it echoes Kant's description of the powerlessness that arises when one experiences the sublime. To experience grace, for Metz, is to be wholly "impoverished" before God, to have nothing to boast of before God, to have lost all of our previous (legal, social, political, religious, "worldly") labels, and so to be bereft of the identity that we had thought defined and secured us. This form of poverty, he finds, is central to the "Christian attitude toward life. Without it there can be no Christianity and no imitation of Christ."[74]

The height of a human acceptance of its state of poverty comes about through a realization, often described as "mystical" in nature, of our "ecstatic poverty" of being. Our poverty, and specifically our embrace of it, is what drives us out from the state of "standing still" (*ek-stasis*) which is also a movement out from the permanent "civil war" (the other meaning of *stasis*) within us, what Paul had referred to as the "inner conflict" between sin and grace (Romans 7).[75] In Metz's wording, "Through grace the human spirit overtakes its innate ecstasis and becomes one with it."[76] For Paul, there was an inner conflict between the external formal appearance ("flesh" in Pauline terms) and the inner being ("spirit") of the individual (Romans 7:14-25), what roughly corresponds to the ancient Greek distinction between the political life (*bios*) and the private, home life (*zoe*).[77] This distinction was what had led Paul to determine a "negation of negation" that would lead the individual beyond any legal designation of their being and toward living in a state of grace "beyond" the Law. The connection that I am making here is that the only way to achieve something like grace in Pauline terms is by "going out beyond" the inner conflict of understanding and imagination (bound as they are by certain logical distinctions) and toward a state of existence that dwells beyond such inner conflict, something, I would argue, like a "sublime grace" that Kant had been trying to describe, or a hypernomianism, as Wolfson has phrased it.

It is, in Pauline terms, the emptying of God into the "flesh" of Jesus that overcomes the limitations of law through the freedom found in grace: again, something like a "lawfulness without law" (Romans 8:1-4). Trying to access grace *through* the Law, or the coordinates of our understanding ("human wisdom" in 1 Corinthians 1:13), would not be possible, hence Paul's insistence that the "works" of the Law are not capable of providing the grace of God (Romans 11:6). We push the limits of our understanding to the point where we are thrust out from (*ec*-statically) the threshold between understanding and imagination, the very limit point where Kant had located a sublime experience made possible only through the structural suspension of law. Suspension of the law (of the understanding) becomes then a form of freedom, one made determinate through the imagination's ability to somehow exist beyond the limits of reason—thus signaling too Kant's misunderstanding of religion as that which does not exist merely within the limits of reason.[78]

The "nothingness" of one's "poor infinity and infinite poverty" is what compels the human person to seek out security in the Law, or what Metz calls the option of the Pharisee.[79] Rather than serve as an accomplice in avoiding the innate mystery of our being, as our peculiar form of poverty, we are called by Christ's own *kenosis* (i.e., God's poverty) to embrace the apparent "nothingness" (or nihilism, a form of "infinite poverty") of our being in order to find our truest self, thus only *in* and *through* our human fragility and poverty. As such, this "power of God," as Paul will call it, is an inverted power, one that proclaims the "weakness" of God, or "Christ crucified" instead of our own understanding (1 Corinthians 1:20-31). In this sense, it can only be perceived as taking place on a level akin to the sublime, which disturbs us and displeases us, rather than the beautiful, which rests or calms the individual who beholds it. Hope, as a result, can only be experienced once there is nothing else left to provide security, a wholly negative experience that yet somehow also provides comfort, and is akin to the experience of a negative pleasure felt through the presence of the sublime.[80] This configuration might also explain Walter Benjamin's once cryptic formulation that salvation only exists when there is nothing left to save.

Redefining the Ecstasy of Death

It is no surprise that the image that best symbolizes such an ecstatic encounter with the sublime and the limits of our understanding is death, the ultimate form of human poverty which we cannot fully articulate the experience of and in which seemingly no pleasure is to be found, though it may somehow nonetheless contain the ultimate negation of pleasure that ironically brings a release (or another form of pleasure). It is not surprising that, as with Georges Bataille, many have been fascinated by the possibility of taking pleasure from, and even in, death, and as potentially misguided as such efforts may be at times. As Metz would suggest in such a way as to highlight the death of God that continues to drive the essence of the Christian proclamation, "Death reveals the self-annihilating quality of poverty in all its fullness."[81] The poverty that humans must embrace leads only and always to one's death, a death died with Christ that is somehow also a baptism (or rebirth) into Christ's death, but which is only possible insofar as one can find new life only after renouncing one's right to possess life. It is only through the renunciation of the paradoxical relationship between life and death that one can find new life. A human being cannot simply construct life on top of this paradoxical situation. Only through embracing one's poverty (or "death" in its Pauline formulation) can something like a new life be discovered, though wholly beyond one's ability to control or define it. In this sense, transcendence would only be possible through the self-negation or self-annihilation that takes place in the embrace of one's poverty of spirit, or, as Paul would put it in Romans, one's death with Christ (Romans 6).[82]

What we are left with in these considerations is a sense that the only tradition that would be capable of bearing the sublime encounter would be something like a tradition that is willing to face its own poverty, to enter into its vulnerability, and to promulgate its failure to represent the fullness of the human being as, paradoxically, its only real strength. Though such a tradition would be established in sharp contrast to how many of the world's (especially religious) traditions function, it would be the only way to preserve the marginalized persons, concepts, or even experiences within society that are most often neglected. It may also signal something like the reunion of aesthetics and religion that had been torn asunder in the modern world. What we are searching for, in the end, may be something quite like a tradition that cannot be possessed or safeguarded, much as the Franciscans might have put it in another era. If such a community resembles the "networks of agape" that Taylor had sought to defend within Illich's speculations, then it is perhaps more critical of the organized religious sensibility that Taylor seems to want to defend as well. Perhaps, instead, there is only a minimal community possible, seeded by a minimal theological gesture, though how such a community comes to be, and what shape it ultimately takes, remains to be seen.

4

History

If we are supposed to be oriented toward a horizon wherein theological claims are continuously risking their own identity and any institutional or ecclesial structure is deconstructed from within, how are we to deal with the reality of tradition, the communities formed by such traditions, and the myriad ways of molding the persons that each of us is within the traditions and communities that form us? How is tradition to be at once affirmed as a necessity for human life and language while also critically examined as a potentially deceptive, reductive, and potentially violent phenomenon? And if we are to re-envision community altogether—perhaps even posit something like a minimal community corresponding to a minimal theology—what would such a thing ever resemble?

In order to move closer toward an understanding of how we might accept while also contest both tradition and community, I want to turn toward the key ingredient behind both phenomena and the way in which it functions: memory, specifically the act of memorialization that undergirds every tradition and identity formed within and by both traditions and communities. By doing so, I am hoping to connect the processes of tradition and community with the paradoxical nature of grace and the sublime encounter that certain traditions and communities foster or work to prevent access to through the creation and maintenance of (religious or pseudo-religious) sites of memorialization.

Surely particular sites of memorialization cannot be considered as sacred simply because they memorialize, sentimentalize, or nostalgically reflect upon a particular point of origin, whether it be nationalistic-ideological, religious, part of a specific cultural-heritage, and so forth. Nevertheless, such sites are often difficult to label as purely secular either, insofar as they might function to cement a community's perception of itself. As many such sites are not necessarily aesthetically beautiful, despite whatever efforts architects, designers, curators, or archaeologists put into them, our search for what calls forth an intense emotional response on the part of the one present at the site must rely upon the sense of something like the sublime, as it is brought to bear upon the one who recalls the tragic scope or commemoration of the event or events being memorialized.[1] To what degree a memory can be a moment of sublimity, however, is not entirely clear. For example, we have seen previously how contested the notion of the sublime even is. Whether or not a memorialization should even seek to approximate such a state of sublime encounter with that which lies beyond the limits of both reason and the beautiful has yet to be established. Within such a line of inquiry, another question lingers as well that returns us to the point of our departure: Is the commemoration of a political site of origin a potentially sublime moment that seeks to legitimate political power? And what is the relationship between the sublime and violence, a point that is certainly not moot, especially considering the Kantian example of the sublime as the experience of the military general who overlooks the horrific battlefield yet from a safe distance.[2]

The sublime is experienced as a space from which the vulnerability of humanity, as its ability to be exposed to violence, is revealed as a grounding principle of the constitution of the human being and its faculties of judgment. This is one of the reasons that war memorials, for example, can often be perceived as hallowed or sacred locations. But what exactly is the relationship between such moments of awareness regarding our proximity to violence and the act of memorialization itself, or that which prompts us to reflect directly upon our precariousness and vulnerability yet from a safe distance?[3] And how might a war memorial, as but one significant instance of such processes, stand in stark contrast to a religious site, where a numinous sublimity is invoked as well, though perhaps from a standpoint that counters the memorialization of violence, or with a religious founder who eschews memorialization in any form (as perhaps is the case with Jesus' empty tomb)?

Commemorating Foundational Violence

Beginning with Constantine, Christianity triumphed at the level of the state and soon began to cloak with its authority persecutions similar to those in which the early Christians were victims. Like so many previous religious, ideological, and political enterprises, Christianity suffered persecution while it was weak and became the persecutor as soon as it gained strength. This vision of a Christianity that persecuted as much as or more than other religions is strengthened rather than diminished by the modern Western world's very aptitude for decoding representations of persecution. As long as this aptitude was limited to the immediate historical environment, i.e., the superficially Christianized universe, religious persecution—violence sanctioned or instigated by religion—appeared as a monopoly of that universe.

—René Girard[4]

What we witness within such a history as that presented by the Christian tradition is a feature that underlies the contrast I have alluded to above: here is a contestation of certain forms of Christian memorialization offered at the same time as we recall Jesus' words asking his disciples to repeat his sacrificial act "in memory of me" (e.g., Luke 22:19). Girard's claim is that such an act is not one intended to promote a sense of safety in the face of impending vulnerability, but rather the opposite: that something like the sublime, if we can even still call it that, can only be approached by embracing one's vulnerability insofar as it weakens one and faces directly toward one's own death—a point I tried to drive home in the preceding chapter. It is not capable of constructing a legitimating political narrative through the establishment of its proximity to a point of origin, but is rather one that disperses such claims, or even seeks to dispossess them in some manner. In this weakening of traditional notions of the sublime seemingly encountered in sites that commemorate national power or strength (e.g., war cemeteries that praise the bravery of soldiers in order to reinforce the strength of a political, ideological narrative), we encounter in the Christian narrative a moment of the displacement of such a power that can, as Girard claims, just as easily be rerouted back toward a "monopolization" of its universe and the persecution of those who deviate from the establishment of such violent communal identities.

Within the horizon of such a reversal of power that Christianity introduces to the world lie too, Girard intuits, the paradoxical origins of political power, origins that are as complicit with concealing the violence that they ceaselessly perpetuate, as they are with appearing as the foundational moment in the life of its institutional edifice, in this case the Church. It is for this reason that theologians must continue to illuminate a self-reflexive theology that takes seriously its complicity with the (repressive) violence that is maintained or is contested at its origins. Unmasking the "ritual origin of political power" means likewise unmasking the origins of any constructed "sacred monarchy" founded upon the violent means that refuse to dwell in the only apparent emptiness that remains once violence is renounced.[5] Despite whatever sublime experience awaits a particular memorialization, asking critical, genealogical questions about our relationship to such points of origin and what they promote vis-à-vis our proximity to violence, as well as what exactly the quality of its sublimity consists in is an issue that must remain central to any nascent political theology.

The politicizing of a sublime experience, or the sublime experience of a politicized space, is exactly how Frank Ankersmit describes the historical dimension of human encounters with the sublime. For Ankersmit, the sublime functions as a de-realization of a threatening reality, which "paradoxically endows reality with a presence that is far more real than reality ever was."[6] The sublime historical experience, *as myth*, reaches out from the past to inform our present identity, overcoming the present moment and transforming it into something else entirely.[7] In this fashion, the truly historical sublime experience is the traumatic event within history that mythically still guides us in the present moment, though Girard's critique of such mythological dimensions gives us ample room to distance ourselves from its potential hold upon the dominance or legitimation of present political structures.

Symbolically, the emptiness we are left with when appearing to challenge the normative and ideological dimensions of collective memorialization, and which may appear to many as the absence of any structural or institutional form (its sense of being normative)—any existing tradition or community—that was founded on such commemorations of violence and exclusion, has often led to a fierce historical opposition to any apparent antinomian elements, or that which appeared to be a force working contrary to any established and frequently referenced political point of origin, as we have already seen. The fear of antinomianism, or of a permanently *negative* anthropology or political theology, however, is that such a view fails to see how a non-teleological eschatological horizon for justice can be a point of orientation as strong, if not stronger and more just, than a politically legitimating story of origins. Nonetheless, such a contrast is often what contentiously fractures a good number of ecclesiologies in that it is often easier, and more politically expedient, to centralize authority through a myth of origins—and its sacral memorializations—than to orient oneself toward an unknown horizon in expectation of a coming encounter. The former option would seem to entail a weakening of any recognition of the Holy Spirit whom the Church is left with to guide it once Jesus ascended to heaven, leaving the Church at times seemingly without a structure by which to identify itself. That is, it is left to abide by a mimetic (or imitative) rationality that would posit a firm identity through enacted ritualistic violence or persecution. Again, such a critique is not to suggest that we can or should permanently leave behind all stories of origins or mimetic, imitative desires (a point that Girard himself had struggled to articulate in his own work); rather, every origin or mimetic desire must be (counter)balanced with a non-teleological horizon as its true "telos" (to use Paul Ricoeur's phrasing of such matters).

The Eucharistic memorialization, for example, done "in remembrance of me," as Jesus had put it, is an act that subverts the linkage of violence and political origins, instituting a political theology that is constituted, not in a Schmittian sense as legitimating sovereign rule, but on the basis of critiquing the alliance between violence and communal identity. Girard highlights such a precise reasoning through, for example, the Gospel narratives' refusal to construct a tomb or memorial structure after Jesus' death.[8] In his blunt assessment, "Murder calls for the tomb and the tomb is but the prolongation and perpetuation of murder."[9] Effacing such memorials as we find in the tomb calls forth a critical discourse on the nature of memorialization—but also any tradition founded on this memory—and the ways in which violence often subsists in the act of commemoration. What Girard's observation points toward, rather, is the unconscious dimension through which society constructs its point of origin through the memorialization that denies the violence that it actually needs in order to legitimate its rule. In his words,

> The very murders in which the fathers directly took part already resemble tombs to the extent that, above all in collective and founding murders but also in individual murders, men kill in order to lie to others and to themselves on the subject of violence and death. They must kill and continue to kill, strange as it may seem, in order not to know that they are killing.[10]

Giving renewed scope to Jesus' reminder that "they know not what they do" (Luke 23:34), we see how the "act of concealment," as Girard will call it, or hiding the violent death, is "essential" to these acts of honoring the dead.[11] This form of invisibility that is cast upon the violent origins of society (but even of some historical-ecclesial structures, one might argue) is what he considers to be the "tomb-religion" that lies at the base of all society, "their only reason for existence."[12] We are chillingly reminded that, socially speaking, "the murder and the origin are the same thing," and the sublime experience cast in mythological terms, as Ankersmit reminds us, may be the link that guarantees its identification in this way.[13] Girard is even at pains to describe how this is not a metaphorical usage of the tomb, but an instance of noting the actually existing physical graves that do mark our world and which are literally denied their existence and (violent) purpose through the absence of a tomb in the story of Jesus' resurrection. Such tombs are not metaphorical, but they do function analogously to bring the past ideal (soldier, patriot, martyr, hero) into the present—a significant contrast between metaphor and analogy that I will return to in a moment.

The question that I believe we must take seriously from within a theological perspective in order to undo such violent associations and analogies is this: Can a sacred site serve, instead of being a memorialization of violence, as rather a reminder of what Ricoeur has called a "critical history," a suspension of history perhaps somewhat akin to what Benjamin considered to be a "weak messianic force" moving within history, or what Metz has designated in a theological context as a "dangerous memory"? How might we understand the existence of such sites as forces of counter-violence and how might they critique other, violence-condoning monuments? What sense of the sublime is accessed through their possible existence and how might this provide a radical critique of violent power relations in our world? Or, more to the point, can the sublime ever be said to exist in a concrete, historical form such as any tradition or community would seem to provide?

Monumental and Critical Histories

Ricoeur turns to the causes of what we experience as the fragility of identity within specific instances of manipulated memory in particular in his *Memory, History, Forgetting*, listing "the heritage of founding violence" as being perhaps foremost among them. As he renders things, while also giving us a general sense of the divisiveness of such acts involving the commemoration of violence,

> It is a fact that there is no historical community that has not arisen out of what can be termed an original relation to war. What we celebrate under the heading of founding events are, essentially, violent acts legitimated after the fact by a precarious state of right, acts legitimated, at the limit, by their very antiquity, by their age. The same events are thus found to signify glory for some, humiliation for others. To their celebration, on the one hand, corresponds their execration, on the other. It is in this way that real and symbolic wounds are stored in the archives of collective memory.[14]

The "state of right" that Ricoeur speaks of is the legitimating principle of national, communal identities, ones shrouded in the founding violence that such communities have made justifiable through the official declaration, implementation, and the apparent sacred duty of war. Despite the all-too-obvious reality that every act of war—when read from the perspective of the war's end—inherently divides those locked in competition into camps reserved for those who experience the glory (or sublimity) of victory and those the humiliation of loss, war is endlessly commemorated as a self-legitimating act (and so acting to legitimate the sovereign) that becomes embedded in the "archives of collective memory," which are themselves preserved through memorial sites, museums, educational curricula, and so forth: "A history taught, a history learned, but also a history celebrated. To this forced memorization are added the customary commemorations. A formidable pact is concluded in this way between remembrance, memorization, and commemoration."[15] The all-pervasive ideological narratives of a given community are "thus placed in the service of the circumscription of the identity defining the community."[16]

Ricoeur's analysis in the context of memory overlaps in a significant way not only with Girard's insights but also with Ricoeur's own commentary on acts of "monumental history" in the third volume of his series *Time and Narrative*. By pointing toward this specific linkage, I want to demonstrate how an alternative account of history, what he will call a "critical history," may be the only way for something like a genuinely sacred history (as a potential "iconoclasm" within history, in his formulation) to be communicated.

Ricoeur's discussion of monumental and critical histories takes place in the context of Nietzsche's second "untimely meditation" on history, which divides history up into its antiquarian, monumental, and critical phases, each seemingly in need of the other to provide a comprehensive portrait of human historical understanding. Monumental history, as the name implies, depends upon the insistence of an apparently "timeless" reflection on the greatness of certain persons within history, those whose fame has resulted in the construction of mausoleums to house them.[17] Such a history has a certain overlap, Ricoeur notes, with Gadamer's sense of "the classical"—a concept central to David Tracy's eventual articulation of the analogical imagination in light of the canonical development of classical texts—an insight I will return to shortly. At the same time, however, Ricoeur is also somewhat critical of analogical methods in light of the tasks that monumental history seemingly places before itself:

> The secret vice of monumental history is that it misleads through the force of analogy, by the very fact that it equalizes differences and disperses disparities, leaving only the "effect in itself," which is never imitable, ones such as are celebrated by our great holidays. In this effacing of singularity, "the past itself suffers damage [*so leidt die Vergangenheit selbst Schaden*]."[18]

The caution we are issued in this regard is that a form of history that wishes to commemorate certain historical acts by turning them into timeless monuments to particular persons, events, or acts within a given cultural memory must level the differences or anomalies that do exist between the monument being remembered or conserved and the actually existing historical figure or event, which is never as neatly presented in history as its memory. This "effacing" of the "singularity" of the person or event is accomplished by this act of analogizing and as such it "misleads" us into positing a more accurate historical memory—something which can never actually be achieved once and for all.

Ricoeur's reading of Nietzsche's critique of monumental history as pointing a way toward the necessity for a critical form of history that probes deeper into the reality of any singularity (as person or event) aids both thinkers in developing a position for historical accounts to deal with the necessity of forgetting, what Ricoeur will call a "happy memory" that must forget things in order to function in the present.[19] This runs counter to the processes of monumental history which analogously brings the past into the present to legitimate certain political goals and foundations. Such a contrast goes a long way too toward explaining not only his development of a critical history but also why Ricoeur maintains reservations about the use of analogy in his magisterial study *The Rule of Metaphor*.

In short, as it takes up the issue in this particular context, the dialectic between poetry (as manifest in something like the sublime) and speculative thought is really a playing out of another tension—one very close to Girard's heart as well—"between the experience of belonging as a whole and the power of distanciation that opens up the space of speculative thought."[20] In this tension, we have made clearer for ourselves the nature of political discourse as rooted in a sublime object that it utilizes for political ends—again, what Žižek had called the sublime object of ideology.[21] What is made clear is that the division between thought and (sublime) feeling is one that opens up a political field of tensions and of one element trying to subordinate the other within the dualism they inhabit (and which constitutes the field of relations, or representations, that make up the sphere of the political, as we have already seen repeatedly). We find this same insight, though in slightly different form, in Nietzsche's reading of history as a tension between the strong and the weak, as well as in Jean-François Lyotard's discussion of the victim within the differend, his term for two meaningful phrases locked in an unresolvable dispute.[22]

It is on these grounds that Ricoeur critiques those traditional arguments for the analogy of being (*analogia entis*) which attempt to create a science of theology and hence to sever theological reflection from the poetic altogether, likewise denying the dialectical tension that gives rise to metaphorical thought in the first place and creating an ontotheology in its stead.[23] By refusing metaphor, those searching for an ever stricter definition of the *analogia entis*, he claims, are not only missing out on the legitimate role of the poetic (or sublime) within thought, but are working at a remove from the tensional truths that govern thought on the whole. They are perhaps even inserting a false form of the sublime encounter within a matrix of representations that relies upon a past point of origin to legitimate present political relations.

Perhaps it could be argued that Ricoeur is missing out on the fullness of those possibilities for understanding that analogy brings us, specifically in the sense we find, in John Milbank's reading, a Thomistic version of a "mediating analogy" that can account for both difference and similarity,[24] or David Tracy's preservation of the "analogical imagination" as a play between analogy and negative dialectics. To preserve the utility of analogical reasoning, despite its tendency to monumentalize history, is to hold out the chance for an aesthetic encounter with the beautiful and not just the sublime—a point that Hans Urs von Balthasar's theological aesthetics alongside his defense of the analogy of being should remind us of. In the words of David Tracy, there is a certain dialectic between analogy and a negative dialectics that too might preserve—

though he does not say as much in this context—the relationship between the beautiful and the sublime. Negative dialectics, which maintains a desire to go (metaphorically) "beyond" whatever identities seem to bind us through a negation of the first, categorical negation that established representational identity in the first place,[25] provides the permanent critique to analogical reasoning that can only be complimented by the way in which analogical thought provides a concrete platform for a shared understanding that a purely negative dialectics cannot:

> Without the ever-renewed power of the negative, all analogical concepts eventually collapse into the false harmony, the brittle sterility, the cheap grace of an all-too-canny univocity or an unreal compromise pleasing no one who understands the real issues. Without the similarities produced through differences and negations, without the continuities, the order and even the possible, actual *or* proleptic harmony produced by an internal theological demand for some new mode of analogical language, negative dialectics, left to itself, eventually explodes its energies into rage or dissipates them in despair. For alone, a theological negative dialectics leads into the uncanny whirlpool of the chaos of pure equivocity: a chaos whose own uncanny *fascinans et tremendum* power must one day discover that its own radicality and liberating power is ultimately empowered by, because rooted in, the same reality as its analogical counterparts: the always-already, not-yet event of the yes disclosed in the grace of Jesus Christ.[26]

It is precisely this unfolding of the analogical imagination, one forged in the back and forth between negative dialectical and analogical methods of reasoning that parallel the critical and monumental histories that Ricoeur had already detected at work in our representational logics, that we might also locate the outworking of something like grace in all of its creative fullness as a shuttling back and forth between the sublime and reason, the poetic and speculative thought, the divine (per chance) and the human, the orthodox and the radical, or law and what exceeds it. This experience of grace is precisely what becomes apparent to us in the ongoing and unceasing dialectic between critique and the monumentalization of the event of Jesus Christ, as Tracy will put it in a strictly theological context.[27]

To what degree grace can be experienced as a form of critique of an already established monumental history is precisely what theology must be seen perpetually to explore, what Nietzsche had drawn close to but recoiled from, and what Ricoeur seems much more willing to circumscribe as the defining biblical expression that theologians are continuously called to take up and champion in whatever context they find themselves. Such an act of critique has the chance to become something like what Miroslav Volf has described as a "perfect love" that "is the goal of memory," the point at which memory is allowed to forget the wrongs that have been done to the innocent—a "formation of the communion of love between all people, including victims and perpetrators."[28] At the least, there arises in response to the existence of a monumental history the need for a "critical history" to appear such that the injustice and unmercifulness of history can be exposed, for, in Nietzsche's words, "every past … is worth condemning."[29]

What Ricoeur is pointing us toward is something like "a certain iconoclasm directed against history, as sealed up in what is past and gone," but which is also "a necessary condition for its ability to refigure time."[30] It is for this very reason a movement against the monumentalizing of history, an *almost* antinomian gesture (that motivates a good many radical theologians and continental philosophers of religion), can easily be mistaken as a heretical affront to the necessity for an analogical, beautiful resonance that lies underneath any established communal identity (the very conjunction that more orthodox theologians continuously seek to defend). What cannot be missed, however, is that such a potential critique *is what actually lies at the heart of all historical-theological reflection*. It is an in-built tension that cannot be effaced, but must be seen for what it truly is. Its orientation toward the future, and not toward a point of origins, is what allows such gestures to be perceived as antinomian, in that they do contest the mythology of legal foundations, though they also rely upon such foundations in another sense (for purposes of shared intelligibility, language, law and society, etc.) while signaling a critique of them from beyond their focus on origins.

The question of whether and to what degree the analogical leveling of differences within the singularity, or singular historical event or person, is a form of violence needing to be removed, or at the least rendered "bloodless," as Derrida would have it, remains to be seen.[31] At the least, we see the need for a critical history, much as Benjamin had once deduced, to suspend the normative workings of history, to "bring dialectics to a standstill," and to champion the one-time "losers" of history, the oppressed and the marginalized, to have their voices heard, perhaps for the first time. In Ricoeur's terms, "No doubt a time in suspension is required if our intentions directed at the future are to have the force to reactivate the unaccomplished possibilities of the past, and if effective-history is to be carried by still living traditions."[32] This is the place where one can locate dialectics at a standstill and the capacity to recall the narratives that were once thought to be lost to history.

We are returned at this point directly to Benjamin's "weak messianic forces" interrupting history in defense of those conquered by history, as well as to Agamben's reading of Pauline thought wherein the messianic, iconoclastic suspension of time becomes a Benjaminian proposition along the same trajectory of thought. This interpretive lineage that I am following would make some sense as well of Ricoeur's reading of memory, as he makes clear in a memorial address on "The Memory of Suffering," that it is precisely our recollection of the lamentations of innocent victims, such as those who died in the Shoah, that distinguishes the murderers (latent within the mythological narrative, from Girard's perspective) from the innocent (revealed, for example, by biblical words and actions): "Is it not the purpose of the [archaic] myths to explain how the whole of reality was brought into existence and, among other things, how evil started? Is it not the basic trend of all myths to look backward toward the immemorial past of the beginning, toward the time of the origin?"[33] In contrast to archaic mythology (and even to the Bultmann-inspired attempts to remove such mythological elements), the biblical narrative is one that promises a release from violent origins and the murders that linger there still. It is an embodied pledge of fidelity to the innocent victims of a monumental history that is in need of revisiting in a more critical light, even if it generates in the end something like Adorno's "inverse theology."

The Critical Idea

Following Gianni Vattimo's reading of the Girardian thesis concerning violence as one that sees the narrative of secularization emanating from the critical history which Christianity unleashes upon every monumental history that would masquerade as a sacred history—and what is often called the mystical, even mythical, origins of sovereign power—we might begin to understand instances of the genuinely sacred within our world as predominantly *critical* in nature.[34] That is, the sacred might be considered as a force that exposes the violent foundations of a given normative order (even in ecclesial terms) in order to condemn foundational or repressive violence. In this reading, there may be a way to read apparently "secular" (even secular political-theological, or, perhaps more accurately, profane) critiques of the apparent sacred within the world as attesting to the manifestation of the sacred in some sense, no matter how iconoclastic or antinomian such gestures may at first appear.[35] Indeed, such thoughts seem to lie at the base of the Jewish and Christian traditions, despite so many centuries of this dynamic being hard to discern under the dominance of apparently monolithic traditions that have tried to conceal such truths.

What we witness through such understandings of memorialization and violence is a deepening of our experience of grace as a lawless law (as we saw in the last chapter), or, as I am here postulating, a forgotten memorial or a memory of the forgotten. In the search for a source that is not a commemoration of the violence that lies at the foundations of society, we are returned rather to a singular presence that can never be fully exposed or explored, but which nonetheless motivates our search for justice amongst those marginalized by history—the face of the individual before us who calls to us and prompts us to leave behind the monumental histories that have justified countless acts of oppression and domination. The singularity we can never describe, but which we always seek to approximate and which escapes the narratives that monumental history provides for us, is the true "source" we are really searching for. In this realization, we are called to focus on the same object Girard has been after—as has Agamben in his study of the figure of the *homo sacer* and the possibility of a form of life lived beyond the law—the fragile and unnecessarily victimized individual whose life needs to be preserved beyond the orders and established communities of this world that reductionistically portray it.

What we are left with in this analysis is the ever-present push toward the effacement of a monumental history that will never completely leave us, a desire for the poverty of theology, or *the Idea itself* arising as an abstraction from the material conditions of existence, hence its weakness to effect political change, but also, paradoxically, its strength to provoke transformation and reform through clearing the space for speculative thought (as the basis of any critique within a given tradition or normative order). In these terms, we are desperately searching for the messianic Idea that arises within religious narratives in order to frame a relationship with material reality, a defense, via the Idea itself, of the alien, orphan, widow, or prostitute, among other marginalized persons, and contrary to the justifications of a more normative violence that works against such persons or groups. What we are after, whether committed to a religious or theological tradition or not, is the poverty of theology (or an "inverse theology") as *the Idea* that takes us above the identities we are given by the social order, and which can never truly be defined once and for all. To embrace this notion is to embrace a negative dialectics ceaselessly at work within any identity or concept, to be sure, but one that must work with its analogical counterpart until the day should arrive when the analogical reduction no longer applies to the reality before us, something perhaps only possible on the day of a certain death—Christ's death, our death, or whatever symbolic death accompanies the end of a given representational world.

The Vulnerability of the Body

To be an historically embodied being, to be engaged in the empirical world that is immersed in history, is to recognize the role of encounter and presence as central to the experience of being human. There is an embodied manner of being in the world that is inherently oriented toward time, and so also history, as Heidegger had once made abundantly clear. To neglect human encounters with presence, whether in the fields of history or religion, encounters with both persons and gods, is to miss one of the most vital components of being human—a hyperbolic excessiveness that transcends the run of the ordinary.[36] To comprehend this point is to comprehend as well why Heidegger's pronouncement of a critique of ontotheology as the end of metaphysics was also what opened up a defense of the metaphysical as that which (symbolically) underlies the foundations of every embodied institution and community. As long as we have communities, with their foundational myths and enthusiastic supporters, we will have metaphysical legitimations given for their existence, despite the accuracy with which Heidegger had criticized such grounds.

As I have already noted, Kant had once tried to ascertain how the historical played no role in determining the boundaries of a rational form of the religious, and his aesthetics seem also to have been developed along these lines, as timeless and so transcendent to the world in which we dwell historically. The sublime would seem to be, from this point of view, at another, further remove from our historically situated being. Yet, I want to ask, can there be an encounter with the sublime that, paradoxically, *brings us back to the historical*, and so also perhaps back to tradition and community? And is this possibility what explains to us Kant's examples of what inspire a feeling of the sublime as typically moments rooted in an all-too-real and all-too-terrifying moments of brutal reality, such as a battle on the field of war or the overwhelming monstrosity of nature? What if our experience of the sublime, rather than taking us away from the historical, returned us to what is infinite *within* history, something like Jean-Luc Marion's saturated phenomena within history that yet evidence the sublime as a part of our historical being? As I have been arguing thus far, I believe that such sublime experiences were what Ankersmit had described as the trauma (*as* sublime historical experience) that returns to us again and again to override our present identity and these may be either, in Girard's terms no less than Ankersmit's, a mythological concealment of our present order's violent origins *or* an encounter that undoes this construction of reality—a de-realization (Ankersmit) or negation (as in Laurence Hemming's work, as we will see) of what had previously maintained our identity.

We can at least glimpse something of the sublime encounter when we reflect on the way that our bodily being, our nudity even, is situated on the borders of what we consider to be beautiful and our access to something beyond the beautiful, as the sublime, through our material bodies. In short, though we typically search to project a sense of the timeless upon the naked human body, our actual encounter with the brokenness of humanity contained in our nudity beyond such projections offers us a glimpse of something like the sublime through our embodied, historical being. As Agamben has put it in his reflections on the exposure of our frail and vulnerable naked selves, "[…] it is precisely the disenchantment of beauty in the experience of nudity, this sublime but also miserable exhibition of appearance beyond all mystery and meaning, that can somehow defuse the theological apparatus and allow us to see, beyond the prestige of grace and the chimeras of corrupt nature, a simple, inapparent human body."[37] There is in this expression something like a purely human grace possible beyond any theologically scripted grace. We can see here the basic contours of Agamben's formulation of a profound disenchantment with the sacred (and its repressed other half, the secular, along with it) which he terms elsewhere an absolute profanation.[38] To move beyond the beautiful, to disenchant it, is to release the individual body from the hold of the theological-political apparatus that bestows its regulated version of grace as an inscription through its fixed and manifest glory. This movement beyond is what allows us to see the human body for what it is, undefinable in its precarious vulnerability. This grace accesses for us a point of sublime encounter that does not legitimate politically oppressive rule, but which points toward our human frailty and vulnerability. In this experience, there is another form of grace operative, but one that cannot be controlled or contained in any human way; it cannot be dispensed by an institution holding it in reserve. It is a wild sort of grace, one that no institution or representation can gain a complete monopoly over in order to dispense it as it sees politically opportune.

Perceived from this angle, the body becomes potentially what Benjamin might call a "moment of danger" within history, the "dangerous memory" that reminds us of the bodies repressed by dominant and totalizing historical narratives.[39] Benjamin's concern that "even the dead" are not safe from the enemy—or the Antichrist who rules over history, as he had put it—certainly reminds us of the vulnerability of the body that which modernity attempted to pronounce dead in favor of an ever-dominant rationality. It also returns us to Ricoeur's reflections on a monumental history that suppress an iconoclastic encounter with a presence within history that we had critically searched for, but which had been so difficult to obtain. The sublime encounter with the other who undoes us and illustrates our vulnerable, precarious selves always takes place in that "model of messianic time," the "now-time" (*Jetztzeit*) that Benjamin and Agamben so steadfastly point humanity toward recognizing.[40]

The question before us now, however, is how the sublime, or even the divine, could be said to exist *meta*-physically, beyond the confines of human experience. There is, of course, a great deal of lingering confusion in contemporary conversations on metaphysics as to whether we genuinely encounter a metaphysical reality when we simply "go beyond" reason or thought in a hypernomian fashion, perhaps also mistaking such an experience as being one with the divine when it is in reality an experience of being at the limits of experience itself, an experience then of reason alone in another sense. This was merely the threshold between thought and the sublime, with which Kant was well familiar. We are as such justified in asking: With what (ontological) reality are we dealing when we contemplate the sublime, which need not be an instance of the divine in our world, but may demonstrate itself as the boundary of human experience? Is it the reality of the divine, or the reality of humanity seen from the edges of its own existence?

The Role of Metaphor

Perhaps, as Jean-Yves Lacoste has put it, we *might* find the divine within an experience of our inexperience, manifest at the limits of our knowing anything at all, through what he calls a "liturgical reduction" of our being in the world.[41] This approach admits the limits of human experience while also pointing toward the possibility of a transformative encounter with the O/other at precisely these edges of experience. Or, as Jean-Luc Marion would have it, there is perhaps something of the divine present within the excessively saturated phenomena that permeate our lived reality.[42] For Marion, who is very clear on this point, the experience of the saturated phenomena is equivalent to the experience of the Kantian sublime or the Cartesian sense of the infinite—yet it is entirely *in* the material world as much as our experience of such phenomena also points beyond our world at the same time. Of course, the sublime encounter, as Kant himself had understood, might too be one as terrifying as greeting a horrific creature crawling out of a deep abyss, and, as Richard Kearney has noted, such an experience may be an encounter with a monster as likely as it may be with an angel.[43]

To produce a possible critique of the sublime as an encounter with something not inherently divine allows us to wonder as well if this further de-mythologization and de-mystification of the possible divine (or of the "God who may be," to follow Kearney's language once again[44]) nonetheless contains any ontological (metaphysical) presuppositions that might benefit a theological reading of the sublime as a possible moment of genuine grace within our experience. Though there is cause to critique the limits of human experience as not necessarily sites of encountering the divine, it would be an overly hasty conclusion to admit that no such encounters were at least possible within these experiences. Pushed to the limits, human experience of the sublime would seem to be *the* locus of a potentially transformative encounter that contains the possibility of rendering our present identities null and void, offering instead an alternative reading of the present (and, consequently, of *presence* itself). Such an admittance does not solve the larger question, however: Is there a theological grace latent within the sublime encounter that is a disruption of our world from yet beyond it, or is it a purely human grace that we experience without having its source within ourselves? That is, do we contain the source of our own disruption within ourselves, and is this what we might call grace? Furthermore, might we consider whether or not these two things are structurally analogous to one another, though entirely separate in terms of their ontological status, or two sides of the same hyperbolic (metaphorical) experience?

For Kant, of course, the link between the sublime and the divine was direct enough for him to attempt to posit a proof of God's existence through recourse to our experience of the teleological ends of the sublime. In the wake of such a proof's unlikelihood to convince potential believers through the incomplete reasoning of analogy, however, what are we to make in the end of the ontological reality of the sublime in relation to the limits both of language and of our understanding of the divine? Will an analogy of being—the traditional support for belief in the divine—be all that we can rely upon to make such a connection? Or will there be something within the linguistic nature of metaphor itself (as it again stresses the *meta* or beyond) that will nonetheless continue to point to the divine through the fissures and paradoxes that inhabit language?

Jean-François Lyotard once contemplated how the impasse between thought and feeling—the "differend of feeling," as he had put it—was one that seemingly called into existence the appearance of the sublime as one way to engage and describe this impasse. Reaching the limits of thought is where one encounters the sublime, where feeling attempts to present what is unpresentable to thought, but which is nevertheless entirely immanent to our world.[45] This dynamic and utterly human experience is where we discover that the divine is perhaps not encountered in the translation from feelings to thought, but rather what is most pronounced in such an experience is the mystery that human beings are to themselves.

The differend is an interesting and important conceptualization here because it brings together the sublime with the metaphorical nature of language. In essence, a differend is a conflict wherein different regimes of language are represented, creating a situation where there can be no immediate resolution (or litigation) according to the impasse that frames the conflict but which also cannot resolve it. Both sides in the differend are unable to refer to the rules of their own language in order to achieve justice within a given situation, and so the true victim within the conflict ultimately cannot give voice to their status *as* victim. That is, there may be a ruling or judgment rendered that does not take into account the language or discourse of the victim, effectively silencing their protest altogether (as in cases of indigenous peoples' rights or as with testimony of the existence of gas chambers at Auschwitz whose only eye-witnesses all perished). The differend accordingly presents us with the double-bind of both being and *not* being something at the same time—the very definition of metaphor.[46]

Lyotard's account of the differend between thought and feeling as two different discourses that often result in feelings being subordinated to thought, rationality, reason, and order allows us not only to see the political dynamics latent within each cultural or linguistic "clash of civilizations" but also to note the political elements locatable within the experience of the sublime. The sublime signals that an impossible situation is "happening," as Lyotard put it, insofar as the sublime, via the imagination, posits an encounter with a presence that cannot actually be presented to the understanding.[47] In such a situation, one discourse attempts to dominate over another, exposing the feeling of the sublime as an opaque legitimation for its dominance, or, as modernity has repeatedly demonstrated, reason dominates over feelings which cannot produce an object for reason to inspect. As we know politically, reference to a sublime origin of political ideology can easily become the foundation for sovereign rule, just as reason, for its part, attempts to govern the liberalism implicit in modern democratic forms.[48] Ontological discussions of the sublime are subsequently a simultaneous entrance into the discourses of political theology.

We might look in this instance to specific readings of metaphor that take account of its (sublime) ontological properties, especially insofar as they are politically, socially, and religiously determinate. That is, we might note how they appear to overcome their fictive "as if" nature in order to provoke reality to be "otherwise" than it is currently configured. There is no doubt that the power of the Kantian "as if" was quickly de-mythologized by a modern critique of its fictive stance vis-à-vis being (its non-ontological nature). This is what Heidegger's critiques had instantly prompted us to take note of. Kant's distinction between the "as if" (representation) and the "as such" (presentation) of the phenomenal object before our eyes gave rise to numerous modern philosophical quests to discern the true nature of the objects we perceive without presupposition, most notably through phenomenological inquiry. It is also true, however, that reality is shaped through the coincidence of invention and discovery as they converge within the "poetic feeling," as Ricoeur once described this state of reality in making his insistence on the "rule of metaphor."[49] Exploring the "ontological commitment" of poetic speech as the way through which we encounter an ecstatic experience of language in its appearing to "go beyond" itself, Ricoeur did not hesitate to pronounce how there may still be "something like metaphor-faith beyond demythologization," or, in the terms he was to develop perhaps more in-depth, a "second *naïveté* beyond iconoclasm."[50] Metaphor, as with the sublime (and with both being understood in an entirely immanent sense), could be seen as providing the shape by which we begin to understand how humanity can go beyond the clash of images and words that typically define our representational world, opening us up to something beyond ourselves, even metaphysically.

The use of analogy, which seeks a somewhat direct access to the transcendent, he deduces, is not on par with that of metaphor, which retains both the "is" and the "is not" within the linkages it posits, establishing the sense that it generates a "going beyond" (*meta*) that implicates metaphysics as much as it does language.[51] Analogy rather seems to reinscribe the identities of the two terms at an ontological level in terms of their essence. The quality of metaphor in both being and *not* being something is what will ultimately lead Ricoeur to define metaphor in relation to Aristotle's distinction between actuality (being) and potentiality (not being), or the "polysemy of being" that discloses the poetic as situated entirely on the level of being.⁵² Again, by drawing our attention to the relationship between metaphor and the split in being between actuality and potentiality, Ricoeur signals the presence of the political-theological element within language and the conflict of discourses (as interpretations). As Agamben has made abundantly clear as well, the division between actuality and potentiality (embedded dualistically in political discourse in terms of *auctoritas* and *potestas*) undergirds Western politics on the whole, as well as Western theological discourse on God's being.⁵³

God, Perhaps

The critique of analogy offered through an invocation of the sublime is brought to a head theologically in Laurence Paul Hemming's contention that the sublime does not have to point to an encounter with God, which would actually be a reductionistic view of a God who must surely transcend whatever we define the sublime to be.⁵⁴ The infinite cannot be brought into the finite, either through analogy or through sublimity (here understood as metaphoricity). By devaluing both approaches, Hemming is able to conceive of the sublime rather as "a name for transcendence as such" and as bound up with an act of negating whatever identity we posit as a unified essence.⁵⁵ This is also, as I am here arguing, the very idea of metaphor that we need to consider. The analogy of being had previously served to suture together a series of temporalities (the past and the present) that cannot really be brought into harmony, a point that modernity's conception of the sublime had only temporarily delayed unveiling. Hence, Hemming can conclude that "with the death of God and the bringing to a close of the divine end of sublimity, comes the end of the operative force of the *analogia entis* which proved to be the product of an impasse, a 'solution' to the divergent temporalities of man, of God and world."⁵⁶ By positing the sublime not only as something to be overcome but also as the negating force of identity, Hemming defines the sublime as an act of transcendence (in the realm of metaphor) while also negating it as a specific (ontological) site of encounter with the divine (in the realm of analogy).

The establishment of metaphor as a process of both abstracting and concretizing within a historically given cultural-linguistic context brings Ricoeur to the point of forming a hermeneutics that takes the metaphorical qualities of ontology seriously.[57] Hermeneutics, the unending task of making an interpretation while simultaneously being caught up in a clash of interpretations, is one that is founded upon the ability of the imagination to "go beyond" the limits of our understanding, a task that Ricoeur grasps through Kant's development of this dynamic in his third *Critique*. In so many words, he considers how, "[…] where the understanding fails, imagination still has the power of 'presenting' (*Darstellung*) the Idea."[58] This basic insight is what will allow Ricoeur to conclude that speculative discourse "[…] bases its work upon the dynamism of metaphorical utterance, which it construes according to its own sphere of meaning."[59] There is, in this power, a "hidden dialectic" between belonging and distanciation that allows speculative thought to appear in the first place—a point that, I would argue, frequently lies unstated in Girard's work as well.[60] There is also a dialectic between the understanding (posited through analogous reasoning) and the imagination (determined as metaphorical thought) that we cannot escape, though we may emphasize one side to the detriment of the other. Trying to legitimate God's existence, or to comprehend it, based solely on analogy, then, is to miss the larger dialectic and perhaps also to do a reductionistic disservice to whatever the divine is imagined to be.

The minimal theology that is present in the end is one that restores the space for theological inquiry in the form of the *Idea* itself, the imaginative transcendence, speculative abstraction, and analogical resources of our immanent and embodied existence. This tension between the Idea and the body, as between analogy and metaphor or the beautiful and the sublime—as also between any given tradition or community and the utopian radical who seeks to undermine them in some sense—is one that cannot be effaced as it is part and parcel of being human. There will always be a shuttling back and forth between them in order to establish the position of the defined self, just as there will always be a utopian challenge given to every established community.

In order to preserve the space of critique itself, of the Idea, there must be a firm distinction drawn between tradition and community, on the one hand, and the sublime encounter, on the other. One's experience of the sublime, perhaps even of existence of the divine, cannot be fixed once and for all in the languages of either tradition or community. The utopian desires for a better world cannot be fully embodied, much as traditional theologians had acknowledged in setting a sharp distinction between the Church and the Kingdom of God. One cannot be defined by the other, though an interaction between them was essential to the definitions of both. These are the dynamics that have brought us this far in humanity's quest to establish itself, and they are the dynamics that will continue to drive the speculative debates between those seeking to defend both identity and community and those looking to lessen the oppressive hold of sovereign power upon those marginalized elements living within. Understanding the permanent existence of these tensions might also enable us to re-examine the role that violence plays in our world today.

5

Violence

The potential realization of the Kingdom of God has been presented historically as many things, including as a revolutionary political act (stressing its *discontinuity* with existing conditions), but also as a guiding light for the reform of currently existing religious and institutional structures (hence rather stressing its inherent *continuity*). Though the Kingdom of God was not to be, and should not be, aligned directly with the institutional structure of the Church or with any already existing kingdom, there is no doubt that the Kingdom of God has been perceived as an ideal or utopian principle which the Church strives toward becoming, while realizing that such a community can never really be achieved in this world.[1] In many ways, the Kingdom of God functions as a permanently unsettling notion of what the Church is not and cannot ever be, but which it strives to approximate in ever-closer terms. This formulation of things runs parallel to the reality of how, when a particular theological discourse finds itself in need of loosening up the staid, traditional norms that have become oppressive to some, the temptation to recall Jesus as a revolutionary agent or as a "dangerous memory" to political, social, or religious structures comes across as almost a necessity.[2]

We see such tensions played out, for example, when we inquire as to whether the Kingdom of God is to be considered as a complex network of relations centered on fostering a sense of love, or agape, thereby slowly reforming society from within (as Taylor has suggested), or as a radical overthrow of existing political and theological relations, a more radical notion to be sure, but one that has found a wide audience in more recent memory. We can also note these tensions, with a stress placed on the language of continuity/discontinuity, in the struggles for authority within the post-Vatican II Catholic Church, where such distinctions often serve as indexes of one's position vis-à-vis the need for either the preservation of tradition or its reform. Though such tensions may be constitutive of the ambiguous foundations that ultimately underlie Christianity (H. Richard Niebuhr's ultimately unresolvable typologies for "Christ and culture" come readily to mind in this context[3]), I want rather to analyze the ambiguity of the term *violence* itself as it is utilized politically in order to either prevent self-reflexive structural reform (hence often used to label certain acts as "revolutionary" and therefore as "violent" when they are in fact reform-based) or champion utopian revolutionary hopes when a particular reform agenda appears to be connected to a "violent" system of oppression.[4] Doing so, I believe, can assist us in discerning just how a critical, self-reflexive awareness within ecclesial structures might be concretely obtainable, while also allowing us to build further off of Agamben's analysis elsewhere of the political dynamics underlying both the Kingdom and its accompanying glory.

Revolution and Reform

A psychological tension between obedience to the structures that be, structures often guarded over by institutionalized "priests," and a "prophetic" disobedience to those very same institutions in order that a more just order might evolve is, of course, an age-old dualistic tendency that is utilized not only for psychological purposes but also for explicitly political ones.[5] In a Kantian sense, our minds are quickly enabled through such tensions to access a representational matrix of intelligibility through easily constructed dualisms.[6] Indeed, such a contrast neatly plays into the "friend" versus "enemy" dualism that characterizes all politics, according to Schmitt, as we have already seen.

Nonetheless, attempting to remove oneself from such a dualistic framework proves to be endlessly difficult, and this despite the great trouble and conceptual nuance often taken toward the possibility of transcending such dualities.

An attempt to transcend our political, dualistic formulations of violence was however given to us by Walter Benjamin at the beginning of the last century in his short essay "Critique of Violence." Conceptualizing a form of "divine" violence as a suspension of a normative political order akin to a worker going on strike, Benjamin introduced the possibility for violence to be understood as a "messianic" suspension of structural forms of oppression, specifically those enacted through the existence of law. The realm of law, as we have generally experienced it, rests upon a dualistic division between lawmaking and law-preserving violence, a tension that appears to exhaust the limits of what forms of violence might be possible in our world.[7] Though the potential for a "divine," "pure," or "bloodless" violence to exist as a messianic suspension of law, and so upend the dualism of violence that remains foundational to politics, is a difficult one to determine, we can nonetheless deepen our understanding of the relationship between violence and the (state of) exceptionality that often underlies its usage through Benjamin's analysis. Benjamin had inherited the discourse on exceptionalism said to lie at the heart of politics from Schmitt, and it is through this appropriation specifically that we see a new potential open up for comprehending political and institutional structures in our world as they are founded upon, and given their legitimacy by, the state of exception that establishes sovereign rule.[8]

Getting ahold of the reality of "divine" violence, however, has not proved so easy to do. The search for a position that would enable us to view violence anew, perhaps indebted to Benjamin's legacy, is something that we see further advanced in the work of Hannah Arendt, for example. In her short work *On Violence*, she calls into question the "obviousness" of violence, or the manner in which history typically takes violent action as part and parcel of simply being human. That is, violence has mainly been an unquestioned response seen as necessary to human survival as well as political order. What is needed, she argues, is a more nuanced vocabulary concerning violence, power, authority, strength, and force, one that allows us to see how power, which is actually given to a ruling order *from* the people, is opposed to violence, which cries out as the last impotent action of those whose power is fading.[9] In her rhetorically effective conclusion, "The extreme form of power is All against One, the extreme form of violence is One against All."[10]

By calling for these distinctions to be made and implemented concerning our understanding and use of violence in the world, Arendt directly challenged modern notions of progress which were either illusions or ideological constructs seeking to legitimate Western, colonial rule.[11] To subvert such a linkage of thought and political power, she focused on the nature of how revolutions come to be and through what violences revolutions might be said to overthrow oppressive regimes. What she discovered, based on the dimensions for violence and power just noted, was that revolution, if arising from the power of the masses, was generally *opposed* to violence, which was more often utilized as the means by which to maintain an oppressive, and so non-powerful, institution. Revolutions are made possible by a breakdown in power, by the loss of forms of civil obedience which are merely a sign of the people's belief in the power they themselves are legitimating.[12] As long as the people who grant power to a given government or institution believe in the effectiveness of such structures, they comply with its organization. The moment such power erodes, the institution fails to command the respect and obedience of the people and can only be maintained through the imposition of violence.[13] In her words,

> Power springs up whenever people get together and act in concert, but it derives its legitimacy from the initial getting together rather than from any action that then may follow. Legitimacy, when challenged, bases itself on an appeal to the past, while justification relates to an end that lies in the future. Violence can be justifiable, but it never will be legitimate.[14]

Through this equation, it becomes possible to see how violence itself never really leads to power (as Arendt defines it) and how the right to rule, as it were, can only be granted through the power given to leadership by the people who are being governed.[15]

Violence "[...] is more the weapon of reform than of revolution," as she had put it, precisely because the temptation to utilize instruments of violence in struggles for power is greatest when an institutional structure is still in place, not once a revolution has exposed the absence of power within those who govern. Violence is the option to be considered when power is being slowly lost, not when all power has flowed away and a revolutionary change of order is sensed to be afoot.[16] But even when violence is enacted, and from whatever side within a given political power struggle, it does not necessarily lead to a revolutionary change of leadership or governance. Instead, as she astutely notes, "The practice of violence, like all action, changes the world, but the most probable change is to a more violent world."[17] True revolution, she wagers, must come about from the power of the people and not from violent acts. In a certain sense, violence is actually in the hands of those who govern the structures that be, while revolutionary violent acts, if truly revolutionary and not simply a minority of persons seeking to overthrow a government for their own dark purposes, rely more upon their exertion of power than upon their ability to enact violence. One can easily imagine within such distinctions the histories of repressive orders and orthodoxies challenged by radical forces looking to alter the institution's sense of self.

Any distinction between revolution and reform must begin with this most basic distinction between violence and revolution. Any institutionalized structure that seeks or is called to reform—and this is perhaps already a crucial difference—must first comprehend whether or not its impulses for reform are generated by the interests of the people (hence "called to" reform) or by those within the hierarchy or leadership of the institution (hence seeking its own reform through a self-reflexive act). This distinction, which of course does not limit the possibility that there may be those on the "inside" of an institution seeking reform for external reasons, might help us to make a further discernment between those "reforms" which are implemented through violent impositions made upon the people—in which case they cease to be reform-based and become instead an oppressive defense of the structures that be—and those which do not impose themselves upon the people, but reflect the power which is bestowed upon the institution by the people, and hence foster reform as an inherently self-reflexive, critical act.[18]

So, how do we avoid simply begetting more and more violence while attempting either to institute reform or to preserve the traditional structures that be? Arendt's original contribution seems to be that we must learn to reformulate the question itself, for the division between violence and power is applicable in either case, and in much the same manner. What I think we can minimally discern in Arendt's study of revolution is that it is precisely at the point where the distinction between reform and revolution breaks down in the crucible of violence that, paradoxically, we might best capture the essence of what allows an institution to maintain itself throughout history: by existing from the power given to it by the people. In such a way, the impetus for reform issues forth from a healthy self-reflexive understanding, one unafraid to critique its own *raison d'être*, that is, to ask itself if it truly and justly serves the people who empower its structures or whether it defends itself for its own sake. In other words, does it allow for a moment of sublime experience to alter its self-definition, or does it seek to exclude such experiences in order to attempt a totalization of its representation of reality?

The Christian Secular

For Arendt, the relationship between a genuine revolution rooted in the power of the people and the concomitant forces of secularization was preeminent, and, in a very pronounced sense, served to isolate the dynamics of the political from the religious. Revolution was a force moving through history that was unleashed in the modern era as never before, not simply an eventual unfolding of "the contents of Christian teaching," she was at pains to stress. Revolution was a force of secularization in particular that was born not through the Reformation per se, but through, in her words, "the rise of absolutism."[19] To be absolute, in the Hegelian sense (as with the historical progression of the "absolute Spirit"), is to be limited by nothing other than one's own self.[20] The phenomenon of absolutism that Arendt speaks of—and though she consistently invokes the rise of absolutism as a force working historically *against* religion—is in many ways the very same principle that worked within, and galvanized, the Reformation. It was what introduced itself as a position that cannot be limited by anything other than one's own self, what must be taken as *absolutely sovereign*, in Benjamin's phrasing.

Arendt seems herself to have been unable to theorize the precise relationship between the absolute and Christianity, as if the former arose of its own accord, within historical modern revolutions that dispensed with centuries of theological efforts to formulate its own absolute foundations and how such conjectures may have played an important role in modern political conceptualizations.[21] If, for example, we understand the Reformation as the repositioning of the absolute, not within the monarch or within any hierarchical, ecclesial structure, but within the individual Christian (and so eventually in formulations of the individual subject), we begin to see how crucial this reformulation of the locus of power was for the modern era. Such a reading would certainly cohere with Foucault's contemplation of modern subjectivity in light of the Western, Christian practices of confession and pastoral power, though the possibility for such a narrative seems to elude Arendt altogether.

The force of secularization that is championed above the Christian impetus for reformation or revolution—and here ironically Arendt follows Martin Luther's reading—demonstrates how the "word of God" now no longer rests within the Church, but addresses all of society and secular government: "[…]

it does not establish a new secular order but constantly and permanently shakes the foundations of all worldly establishment."[22] Though I would perhaps suggest that such a force is not wholly severed from its Christian roots either, but is perhaps bound up within it, even if it takes a separate, secular form at times, Arendt's point is well-taken: there is a force of revolutionary scope at work within "the foundations of all worldly establishment" that seems to have emanated from *within* Christianity itself. The question that remains is to what degree such a revolutionary force could be considered its own, separate form of violence, one apart from the violence that simply seeks to preserve the rule of law. And, again, we are led back to the question of whether or not we are dealing with a genuinely self-reflexive structure and how such a structure eludes becoming the typical structures that define our world. Indeed, perhaps a genuinely self-reflexive structure, in some sense yet to be determined, eludes ever fully becoming a concrete, historical structure at all—more akin to the space for pure thought or the Idea from which all critical thought emanates and which frequently bears the marks of the messianic, as we have already seen. In this formulation of things, we begin to see again why the tension that prevents the sublime experience from ever being historically embodied in a particular tradition or community is so essential to stress: it is precisely what prevents power from seeking an absolute form and so what prevents violence from spiraling out of control in our world.

Divine Violence

Benjamin had indicated that the "pure" or "divine" violence he was searching for as an alternative to lawmaking or law-preserving violence would be more akin to the precise definition of the "sovereign": it is at once not only a political notion but also a theological one that threatens to stand above the realm of the political altogether. Agamben, some years later, and in response to both Benjamin and Arendt who sought for ways to understand our desires to transcend whatever political order was set before us, would search for a parallel form of "revolutionary violence" that, in his words, "casts itself into the Absolute."[23] Agamben, for his part, would be consistently more attentive to the theological inflections which such a striving for an absolute position takes, even going so far at times to demonstrate how Western politics, and its absolutes in myriad form, find their foundations in a pre-existing theological discourse.[24] By doing so, he was to expand our comprehension of political theology by a good measure as well.

Human action, including the communities that it founds, is intended to secure its own foundations since, by definition, its actions are not considered to be according to nature. Sacrificial mechanisms, he reminds us in an essay that takes up Hegel's use of the Absolute as perhaps *the* key philosophical category to be utilized in this regard, are an attempt to ground humanity through violence:

> It is the very ungroundedness of human activity (which the sacrificial methologeme wants to remedy) that constitutes the violent (that is, according to the meaning that this word has in Latin, as *contra naturam*) character of sacrifice. Insofar as it is not naturally grounded, all human activity must posit its ground by itself and is, according to the sacrificial mythologeme, violent. And it is this *sacred* violence (that is, violence that is abandoned to itself) that sacrifice assumes in order to repeat and regularize in its own structure.[25]

If we are seemingly doomed to repeat such foundational, sacrificial, and violent gestures throughout history, there is also an ethical imperative that arises from these considerations that is very much one calling for a "fulfilled foundation of humanity" that does away with both such sacrificial mythologies and their violent mechanisms and the false sacrality that surrounds them (hence too extending both Adorno's and Girard's critiques of mythology).[26]

Perhaps Arendt wavered on a precise definition of the absolute in relation to religion, and even violence, because it is in the very nature of violence to appear as itself an absolute, a proposition that should give pause to thought itself so that we might contemplate how exactly the quest for an absolute does or does not bring about a "revolutionary violence." Jean-Paul Sartre, for example, in his *Critique of Dialectical Reason*, posits that "every violence even is produced, lived, refused, accepted as *the absolute*."[27] Violence, in this reading, presents humankind with the basic question that later came to plague Emmanuel Levinas when confronted with the other before us: "to kill or to be killed."[28] Insofar as this question, *the* question of violence, presents itself as a moment that promises to unite all of the violent forces within one's life, violence appears entirely *as* absolute, as its own foundation or point of origin, as the tautology that grounds sovereignty through its "exceptional" use and the mystical encounter with an authentic presence that is allegedly uncovered by the archaeologist searching for said origins. Here somewhat supplementing Arendt's reasoning, violence is itself an attempt to posit an absolute origin, and not just to defend a given existing structure or institution. Violence provides the illusion that an origin *can* exist *as* absolute. This is where the temptation of a particular religious community to view itself in entirely exclusive terms—as the only community to have a monopoly on truth, for example—stems from, and it is a position that fosters a violence rarely accepted for what it is. This is also precisely what a theology that embraces its own poverty stands opposed to.

What those searching for an absolute stance vis-à-vis sovereign power are looking for are their own foundations, their own point of origin that is beyond reproach or critique. This is the self-determining stance or "mystical" foundations of authority that can never be legitimated, the spiritual quality of dictatorships even, as Derrida had once put it in his critique of Benjamin's views on violence.[29] "Since the origin of authority, the founding or grounding," Derrida had contended, "the positing of the law cannot by definition rest on anything but themselves, they are themselves a violence without ground."[30] The legitimation of the community's social cohesion through recourse to a point of absolute origin—which I would add was often taken to be sacred—was something that Arendt had already noted as opposed to the justifications given for violent action. To quote her again: "Legitimacy, when challenged, bases itself on an appeal to the past, while justification relates to an end that lies in the future. Violence can be justifiable, but it never will be legitimate." What is interesting in this conceptualization of violence is not only how it mirrors Riceour's comments on how we are always situated between an *arche* and a *telos* but also that Arendt's observation is at once able to reveal how violence, which is always ends-oriented, is not capable of providing legitimacy for a sense of social togetherness while also demonstrating that this is precisely what is most often attempted in the political sphere. Political, social, and communal solidarity is in fact often established and maintained unapologetically through violent means.

In such thoughts, we are brought back to Derrida's reflections on the circular reasoning that grounds articulations of power, as well as the fundamental theological question regarding the existence of the Church apart from its indebtedness to the dualistic relations of power that ground both sovereignty and governance: How are we to distinguish between the (false) sacred origins of the Church that unify the members of the Church through violent, sacrificial, and mythological means, and the eradication of such forms of sacrality that pave the way for new forms of the sacred, or even of (self-)sacrifice, to emerge?[31]

It is at this point that we might begin to see why Derrida's intervention concerning the grounds and implementations of violence is so important, for he aims his subtle critique of Benjamin's views on violence toward answering the fundamental question that remains before us: If no origin can be legitimate for violent actions, then what chance is there for justice to be housed within any given structure or institution? Are not all structures inherently corrupt then and needing to be done away with? Should we not simply yearn for the sublime experience that transcends them all? It is with this last question that we face in particular the almost singular issue that the most vocal critics of deconstructionism are often most afraid deconstructionists are taking far too seriously—the seemingly nihilistic destruction of all foundations and the almost antinomian furor such a stance threatens to release, or that which plagues every critical deconstructivist-genealogical inquiry (and which is a major theoretical-critical undercurrent of most radical or "negative" political theologies today).

In Derrida's estimation, justice does not appear within whatever structure or representation we stand before because justice *cannot* ever fully, exhaustively, appear within whatever order or authority is already founded. Existing representations will always appear to be unjust in that the justices which they do actually contain, which are always already at work within them and which hopefully surpass previously unjust representations, cannot ever be fully just or perfected. This does not mean, however, that the invisible workings of justice in any way actually negate the work that justice does, spectrally, from *within* such representations.[32] This force, in a twist upon Benjamin's initial formulation, is also messianic for Derrida, though it cannot become a historical messianism foreclosed in a particular, concrete, or material form, as I previously noted.[33] The messianic hope will only remain the *chance* for justice to be done within any given structure which will always be, and as Arendt demonstrated, foundationally illegitimate. We can only search for justice within such structures and find it to be already present there, always, but also always "yet to come."

The paradox inherent to the establishment of any law is one that highlights the "absolute" nature of both law and violence: the law will always appear to humanity as transcendent of our established material conditions, or as absolute, but it is also only made possible through the entirely immanent and absolute performance by humanity that brings about the law in the first place. This aporia, as Derrida labels it, is absolute in that there is no foundation other than the one that we make for it ourselves (again, an expression of the tautological nature of sovereignty).[34] As such, law-making violence contains within itself a law-preserving violence at the same time; it calls for it and never ceases to do so as the "paradox of iterability," or the capacity for justice to be repeated in each and every institutional structure.[35] Somewhat ironically, it was Derrida the master decontructivist who also called for a defense of canons, structures, and norms in general, as such things cannot simply be done away with just because they contain an inherently fractured or unstable identity. This is a point often neglected by those critics of deconstructivist thought who see in it only and entirely a destructive or nihilistic affair.[36]

Any sort of divine violence, whatever such a thing would actually be, like nonviolence then too, exists outside of the sphere of law or of representation.[37] Furthermore, if God could be said to be "authority, justice, power, and violence" all in one place, then it is as such only "in secret" that they coalesce in the name of God: "It can be called—sovereign. In secret. Sovereign in that it calls itself and it is called there where sovereignly it calls itself. It names itself. Sovereign is the violent power of this originary appellation. Absolute privilege, infinite prerogative."[38] Another way to put this state of affairs, Derrida seems to suggest, is that divine violence does not exist, cannot exist, just as God could not be said to exist *as such*, in concrete, material terms. God, perhaps like justice, might only exist as a spectral presence within any given representation, any given structure or institution, relation or identity. God may exist, but always only "in secret."

Like Sartre before him, Derrida seems to wonder whether there might not be a more proper analysis of violence lurking underneath Benjamin's critique, one that would search for more of the myriad links between one violence and all the rest, "the worst" as he calls it, "because each individual murder and each collective murder is single, thus infinite and incommensurable."[39] This is the absolute nature of violence, and what is felt underneath even the least violent act. It is also not far from where Arendt wandered amongst the terms often conflated together when we talk about violence, authority, force, and power.

What I would argue at this point is that what we see in each theory I have inspected thus far—Arendt, Benjamin, and Derrida—is a search to describe a truly revolutionary action that nonetheless defies typical characterizations of violence, for, as Arendt had already seen, "[…] violence is no more adequate to describe the phenomenon of revolution than change."[40] What the genuinely revolutionary impulse should be after—and here Arendt cites the early writings of Thomas Jefferson who had for his part wanted so desperately to steer people away from sacralizing constitutions—was a permanent process of revolution that would unsettle each and every generation, something like the messianic force Derrida was after that would work from within any given structure or identity in order to see a chance for justice to occur.[41]

Revolutionary Violence

Agamben's engagement with the topic of violence early on in his career, and though clearly indebted to Arendt's work, met with various expansions and clarifications in his later writings as he continued to interpret the thoughts of Benjamin within the context of his evolving *Homo Sacer* project.[42] Agamben, in a rather youthful essay, however, provides us with a vision of something like Benjamin's divine violence established as a "revolutionary" violence that which, I would argue, nevertheless remains an explicit focus throughout his work even though this precise phrase seemingly dropped out of his lexicon shortly after its conception. Revolutionary violence, as a messianic suspension of history yet *within* history, and as the only authentic extension of sacred or divine violence in the modern world, becomes a launching point for Agamben's work in more ways than one, expanding to reach out to his frequent discussions of antinomianism, the role of gesture beyond language, governmentality, and the relationship between life and law in general, or that which leads to his articulation of a form of life lived beyond the confines of law.[43] If seen from this point of view, the trajectory of revolutionary violence has not disappeared from his sight, but has only grown more intensified as it permeates his overall "emancipatory" project.

What Agamben sought to delineate in this early essay in particular was a form of violence that "carries the right to exist within itself," needing no external legitimation and thereby becoming absolute.[44] His critique of Benjamin at this juncture is that the latter had only "half fulfilled" the search for a violence that "contains its own principle and justification," for Benjamin's "pure" violence which sought to suspend the rule of law, and so was opposed to mythic violence which seeks to instantiate law, still expressed a teleological orientation. In Benjamin's account, all law as a form of means was "either lawmaking or law-preserving," a distinction that Agamben wishes to open up through the consideration of a form of "pure" or "divine" violence that avoids what appears to be the only option for a means-, and not ends-, oriented violence.[45] That such a "divine" violence might take place through a messianic or revolutionary suspension of normal rule is what aligns not only Benjamin's "Critique of Violence" with his eventual theses on history, which further develop the notion of a "weak messianic force," but also what unites the conceptualizations of violence and the messianic within Agamben's own development of revolutionary violence.[46]

Following Arendt, as well as Benjamin, Agamben develops a notion of revolutionary violence that seeks to respect how power is fundamentally different from violence, one that "deliberately refrains from enforcing law, and instead breaks apart the continuity of time to found a new era."[47] It is the quest for an action to take place outside the bounds of law or representation, one that mirrors the minimum level of revolutionary or sacred activity that he will seek to develop—and though he will later substitute the word "profanation" for revolution.[48] What is central to remember concerning the overlap between profanation and revolution in particular is that it draws its analysis in contrast to Arendt who had seen the convergence of revolution and the forces of secularization as that which keeps us wholly within the immanent sphere of the political.

What we encounter in divine violence is instead something like the suspension of the suspension (or "state of exception" that, according to Schmitt, had mythically founded the rule of law). Divine violence does not remove the guilt of the guilty, so to speak; it rather removes the law that imposes such guilt in the first place.[49] In this fashion, the entire sense of order and meaning that is given to our world through an imposed providential or "theological" worldview is rendered "meaningless," *as if* without meaning. In the words of Žižek, who offers us this insight in his reading of Benjamin's notion of divine violence, what is revealed through such a gesture is a form of sovereignty understood as an expression both of divine impotence and yet also of love.[50] Love enters the discussion precisely because the event that characterizes divine violence takes place as a decision "[…] made in absolute solitude, with no cover in the big Other. If it is extra-moral, it is not 'immoral,' it does not give the agent license just to kill with some kind of angelic innocence."[51] Recalling Kierkegaard, such violence is a "work of love" in that it has no structural support or state approval, but issues forth from the desire for justice alone. In this sense, it appears as neither sacred nor profane, but as outside the sphere in which such divisions are established—what Agamben was actually trying to describe in his use of the term "profanation." In this manner too, Žižek sounds a lot like Derrida who had removed God's existence from the equation (it is only "in secret" or with an "impotence" that we see God), but preserved the possibility for justice to emerge as the only language through which we can speak of violence (and perhaps even of love).

For Agamben, any authentic revolutionary act must be one that takes place on the level of profanation, stemming from neither a false sacrality nor a secularization that merely represses the (false) sacred but allows it to flourish in other ways. In terms that immediately seek to grasp what is at stake politically within the tension between the secular and the profane, Agamben declares: "Once profaned, that which was unavailable and separate loses its aura and is returned to use. Both are political operations: the first guarantees the exercise of power by carrying it back to a sacred model; the second deactivates the apparatuses of power and returns to common use the spaces that power had seized."[52] Though he does not use the word "revolutionary" in this context, it is theoretically consistent with his earlier usage and the only apparently obvious way in which to describe the political consequences that follow from this difference.

Though Arendt had shied away from positing such a process within the origins of Christianity, Agamben gravitates closer to this possible religious source, locating the suspension of political machinery—or rendering the political apparatuses as "inoperative," in his terms—in the theological understanding of Jesus' disruption of the sacrificial (mythological) mechanisms and its calling into question the very boundary between the sacred and the profane.[53] What we can find present within the Christian narrative, and as startling a conclusion as one might find concerning a religious reading of the divine, is the paradoxical insistence that "an absolute profanation without remainder now coincides with an equally vacuous and total consecration."[54]

To suggest as much is to provide what has been called by Žižek the "supplement" to Agamben's thoughts on profanation. Žižek's contention is that an act of profanation, "as a gesture of extraction from the proper life-world context and use," is precisely what we should consider as also being an act of sacralization, the only true materialist conclusion to be drawn from this act of profanation.[55] That is, the zero level of the sacred is actually a clearing of the ground upon which the false sacred had been established. In this manner, what Žižek contemplates, and what we see too running as a strand throughout Agamben's thought if viewed from this same angle, is that it is Christianity that introduces the idea of a God who "profanes himself" so to speak, though this act is undertaken so that we might return to another form of sacrality in the end.[56] This idea has of course gained a lot of currency lately in certain philosophical "returns to religion," and in various readings (including Žižek's) of Girard's cycle of violence, and it is one that we need to pay much closer attention to, though it is also one that is due further theological investigation. This line of inquiry does strike a chord, I would argue, that runs parallel, politically, to Dimitris Vardoulakis' point that sovereignty is not opposed to democracy, but serves as a supplement to it, one that cannot be eradicated from the realm of the political altogether.[57]

Relying upon the work of Jean-Pierre Dupuy, who himself interprets the work of René Girard on violence and the sacred, Žižek notes how Christianity introduces a radical critique or "demystification" of the sacred that also radically destabilizes the social cohesiveness of communities dependent upon mechanisms of scapegoating and violence that had previously served to unite them.[58] For Girard, who truly takes center stage in this context theoretically, and though Žižek refrains from citing him directly, the death of Jesus was the ultimate critique of the false, archaic, and violent forms of sacrality that haunt our world to this day, ones reliant upon the act of scapegoating false victims in order to secure a sense of internal coherence within its community. The liberation of humanity from such cycles of violence is what places Christianity, in its rejection of such forms of "sacralized" bonding, closer to contemporary forms of atheism or secularism than many might suspect.[59] In Girard's own words, "The Cross has indeed transformed the world, and we can interpret its power in a way that does not have to appeal to religious faith. We can give the triumph of the Cross a plausible meaning in a completely rational frame of reference."[60]

Girard's main contention is that the Christian narrative's power to demystify the false sacred illuminates the (Pauline) "paradoxes of the Cross" that much more clearly.⁶¹ Žižek's use of Girard in order to highlight the paradoxes of an immanent materialism—that it is "not all" or "less than nothing" to itself—may, as he also reads Agamben, open up a space for the sacred to reappear, though, like Derrida, this conclusion too signals the end of philosophical or political speculation, and so a great silence descends within their work regarding the actual nature of any alleged form of sacrality. What is noteworthy in this context is that the sacred has only a negative currency from this perspective, which is perhaps for many the point at which philosophy must leave things.

An Ontology of Poverty

Returning to the context of violence specifically, Agamben had considered how revolutionary violence runs parallel to instances of ritually repeated sacred violence which tear apart "the homogeneous flux of profane time."⁶² The attempts of these "primitive peoples" through their ancient religious practices to bring about a moment of "primordial chaos" will actually in many ways mirror his later discussion of the Pauline defining of *kairos* as a moment wherein the divine ruptures the historical flow of time much like the force of the sublime or the entrance of the Kingdom of God into our world.⁶³ What follows from such a reading is nothing less than Agamben's most pivotal and instructional understanding of identity: that the only genuine way to comprehend the subject is through the division of one's socially constituted, but for that reason *already divided*, identity. This "division" of any pre-existing social division, as the "division of division itself" he reads as active in Paul's letters, and as I have already discussed it, becomes not only a profound theological reading of the Hegelian-Marxist "negation of negation" but the basis for the cancellation of any identity whatsoever while also somehow preserving it at the same time.

In this early essay on violence, he pronounces much the same process, for it is only those forms of revolutionary violence that are willing to negate their own identities that "[…] may aspire, as revolutionaries always have, to call a messianic halt capable of opening a new chronology (a *novus ordo saeclorum*) and a new experience of temporality—a new History."[64] Though Pauline thought will force us to consider this "new secular order" as somehow too a new form of sacrality, one that brings about a new understanding of the sacred through the apparent profanation of sacrality, Agamben will, in this context, simply aver to the political implications of such conjectures. Relying on Marx's formulation of the revolutionary class as the only group which is capable of negating itself "in the negation of the ruling class,"[65] he states:

> Revolutionary violence is not a violence of means, aimed at the just end of negating the existing system. Rather, it is a violence that negates the self as it negates the other; it awakens a consciousness of the death of the self, even as it visits death on the other. Only the revolutionary class can know that enacting violence against the other inevitably kills the self; only the revolutionary class can have the right (or perhaps, the terrible imperative) to violence.[66]

The comparison of such an act of negation to something like sacred violence is only further cemented by Agamben as the act he searches for is somehow both sacred and revolutionary, as it involves the act of self-negation at the same time as it invokes self-sacrifice. "Repressive" violence, by contrast, is that which not only serves to legitimate the rule of law, but that which proceeds by negating the other without negating the self—the very definition of oppression. The violence that he seeks to isolate beyond the regressive form is therefore at once revolutionary, but perhaps also *sacred*, especially if we take seriously the claims we have already seen of both Benjamin and Žižek. Here we can easily detect the fluidity between the orthodox preservation of an established order and the radical deconstruction of its autonomous structure. It is the negation or division of the *self* (and *not* the other) that introduces a certain "weakness" or poverty into history, but it is also the only chance for oppression to be lifted from this world. This "ontology of poverty" is the only thing that can point toward an understanding of time beyond what the flow of historical time can offer us, an interruption that contains a significant opening toward the theological, but which cannot cross over into its domain.

At this early point in his career, Agamben laid the foundations for his later efforts to point toward a realm beyond language, as through gesture and as toward the domain of the sacred, a space "which radically disturbs and dispossesses humankind."[67] It is a radical, even revolutionary space where all the normal mechanisms by which we structure or legitimate our world are suspended and wherein too our identities break down so that life itself might be found lurking deep underneath. As I have been noting all along as well, I would even venture so far as to suggest, along with Žižek, that something of the sacred might be said to be preserved in this formulation of things: "The living cannot recognize their own essential proximity to death without negating themselves, and this contradiction acts as the seal guarding the most sacred and profound mystery of human existence."[68] If this sounds akin to some of the oldest formulations of where divine justice could be said to thrive, it is no mistake. The prophet, as it were, views the system from the outside, which is to say, from the perspective of its eventual passing away. The prophet sees the potential latent within the structure that is always nonetheless present within it—an inherently self-reflexive, critical act that is somehow still part of the system, providing a view for reform from within its innermost workings.[69]

Theologically, the question for the Church or any worldly institution really, however, is quite clear: Does it present itself as a point of sacred origins and possibly conceal its relationship to violence, or does it reveal the temptation to violence at its core by acknowledging the permanently unresolved tensions that constitute it in the first place? Furthermore, how can such institutions recognize their relationship to a messianic force of profanation that searches for an encounter with that which lies beyond the dichotomy of sacred and secular? And, beyond this, might not the search for an answer point us toward something like the displacement of the tension between law and grace, the very distinction upon which the Church itself was founded?

The Singular Form of Life

In his more recent work, the culmination of the entire *Homo Sacer* series titled *The Use of Bodies*, Agamben continues to press his interpretation of Benjamin's "divine violence" under the heading of a "destituent potential," or "destituent violence," that is a deficient violence that manages to evade the historical-political dialectic between constituted power and constituent power upon which all revolutions are dependent.[70] It is quite simply a violence that does not seek to construct a new law in place of one rendered inoperative; rather it is a violence that "inaugurates a new reality" (much as with his earlier formulation of revolutionary violence) though it is one possibly associated with some form of anarchy as well.[71] Though an immediate critical response to such a suggestion might be one that decries its apparent utopian gesture, Agamben is quick to link such an ontology of potentiality, what he calls a "modal ontology," with Saint Paul's deactivation of social and political identities in his rendition of the messianic suspension of "every power, every authority and every potential."[72] This is what will allow him to so perfectly capture the radical, almost antinomian elements that I have been pursuing throughout this study. Again, as he so painstakingly laid out in *The Time That Remains*, Agamben searches through the origins of Christianity for an alternative logic that reflects what he is after, one that divides every existing social, political, and religious division, rendering each constituted identity inoperative while, at the same time, not entirely doing away with them either—the very move that he will also suggest would allow Saint Paul to famously, and not without some degree of controversy, suggest that he was seeking not to do away with the law, but to *fulfill* it.[73]

> That is to say, the messiah functions in Paul as a destituent potential of the *mitzwoth* that define Jewish identity, without for that reason constituting another identity. The messianic (Paul does not know the term "Christian") does not represent a new and more universal identity but a caesura that passes through every identity—both that of the Jew and that of the Gentile. The "Jew according to the spirit" and "Gentile according to the flesh" do not define a subsequent identity by only the impossibility of every identity of coinciding with itself—namely, their destitution as identities: Jew as non-Jew, Gentile as non-Gentile. (It is probably according to a paradigm of this type that one could think a destitution of the apparatus of citizenship.)[74]

What Agamben is after is a "form-of-life" that "is the revocation of all factical vocations, which deposes them and brings them into an internal tension in the same gesture in which it maintains itself and dwells in them."[75] This specific search helps us understand why he will ultimately find the Franciscan order to be of great interest in *The Highest Poverty*, for it is an order that strives explicitly not to possess things, but only to use them—an outworking of this Pauline logic in concrete, material terms.[76] It is in such historical dynamics that we encounter a minimal theology utilized as an attempt to locate the bare minimum possibility for the sacred within our world.

The Franciscans, of course, had quite a struggle historically to legitimate their existence vis-à-vis the institutional Catholic Church, as they served in some sense as a deactivation of the economies upon which the Church had constructed itself—a point that should only further illuminate the difficulties latent within humanity's reliance upon sacrificial violence as a foundational act, but also the tensions I have been stressing between orthodox institutions and those radical ideas that challenge them. The Franciscan's existence was a protest to the ways in which the Church saw itself within the economies of the world, calling them to accountability as an internally apparent critique of existing ecclesial structures. Their existence also prompts us to consider in what way they are a possible answer to the following question: What might an institutional reality formed in relation to destituent violence look like, for either state or church?

In trying to answer this question, Agamben interestingly does not attempt to advance what many critics of his work, and of genealogical methods on the whole, might otherwise suspect him to advocate: the complete revocation of all institutional forms. Rather, he refers at the end of *The Use of Bodies* to Plato's "Nocturnal Council" from the latter's *Laws*, wherein Plato suggests the existence of a radically heterogeneous body that exists as an "anarchic and anomic element" that acts upon its destituent potential in order to render laws inoperative, not from outside the domain of law, but from *within* it. That such a body might be recognized as a legitimate force operative within an institutional structure it consciously seeks to render inoperative might strike some as mere fancy. However, the outcome of his initial quest for a revolutionary violence might actually be something akin to a permanently revolutionary council *within* a governing body, one that has the power not to construct new laws, but only to render ones already in existence inoperative. That such a body might serve to mitigate unjust laws and perhaps to render social forms of violence less oppressive is certainly worth taking a minute to contemplate. Such a process of contemplation, we might also discover, would allow us a glimpse of just how the social, political, and religious structures of our world are typically constituted in the absence of such an "anarchic and anomic" body.

What these reflections mean for the future of theological investigation, however, is another issue, as the true poverty of theology must consistently search for ways other than through sovereign gestures of authority and autonomy to embody the double negation that typifies the basis of Christian thought. At the very least, what once posed as Christian theology has reached an end that can no longer be paraded as triumphant in any worldly, sovereign sense.

Conclusion

Re-engaging the Secular

What Hans Blumenberg was acutely cognizant of in his *The Legitimacy of the Modern Age* were the dynamics of co-opting theological propositions that secularization conspired in but was more frequently loathe to admit directly. Nevertheless such processes were more than merely an unconscious borrowing from the realm of religion—they were somehow also necessary adoptions for the efficient regulation of social, economic, and political orders. As he would aptly describe things there,

> Expressions of such a generous character, of such a degree of generality and intransitive indeterminacy, are allowed to pass, in our overrich supply of terminology, until almost without arousing notice or suspicion they present themselves in a more precise function. The world that became ever more worldly was a subject whose extension was about as obscure as that of the impersonal "it" in the proposition "It's raining." But in the more precise function, propositions of an entirely different form appear, propositions of the form "B is the secularized A." For example: The modern work ethic is secularized monastic asceticism; The world revolution is the secularized expectation of the end of the world; The president of the Federal Republic

is a secularized monarch. Such propositions define an unequivocal relation between whence and whither, an evolution, a change in the attributes of a substance. The great all-inclusive process of the secularization of the world now no longer appears as a quantitative loss but rather as an aggregate of specifiable and transitively qualitative transformations in which in each case the later phase is possible and intelligible only in relation to the earlier phase assigned to it. What we have here is no longer the simple comparative statement that the world has become more "worldly" but rather, in each asserted case, only the assertion of a specific mutation leading to the specific "product of secularization."[1]

As Blumenberg further catalogs within the modern era, criminal law implies a theological conception of guilt, the tidings of salvation become, in Machiavelli's writings, forms of propaganda, expectations of political redemption are easily perceived as secularized notions of a biblical paradise or as types of apocalyptic messianism, modern ideas of progress stem directly from the story of salvation as signs of providence or fate, and science was quickly portrayed as the combination of world design and those directions for action embedded in historical theological claims.[2] Literature too, especially in the novel form, was to be perceived as presenting its reading audience with secularized versions of those acts of pietistic self-examination that the Reformation brought wholescale into modernity, transforming Augustine's *Confessions* into the prototypical forerunner of the modern autobiographical memoir.[3]

This list is by no means exhaustive. Such revelations regarding the role of secularized theological concepts as Blumenberg notes were, we must add, what had initially drawn Max Weber to suspect a deeper connection between the Protestant work ethic and notions of predestination.[4] Despite the possibility of a "binity" replacing the trinity, the trinity itself, as Giorgio Agamben has masterfully shown, was co-opted by economic models of governance that existed in a perpetual tension with those models of sovereignty that rested upon particular configurations of Christ as King (reintroducing the binity once again).[5]

These connections and transmigrations are, however, merely the tip of a much larger iceberg threatening the theological project of sovereignty. The political dualisms that undergird much of Western politics seem frequently to be predicated on a works/love (or Law/Gospel) dichotomy as old as Western Judeo-Christian thought. One need only look at the contrast possible between a conservative transcendent sovereignty defended in Schmitt's political theology and an opening toward a liberal society of toleration and pure immanence in Spinoza's version, among others, of what an alternative political theology might resemble. In economic and material terms, the focus given throughout the centuries on sacramental realities, relics, and other holy objects is not detached from burgeoning desires for commodified and sexualized fetishes in the modern era.[6] There is a direct link between the submissiveness that was once demonstrated in lying prostrate before the altar of God and contemporary forms of patriotism and consumerism.[7] Moreover, there have been those commentators, following Marx, who have seen how "God is only idealized capital, and heaven only the theorized commercial world."[8]

To note, the secularization of theological concepts that define politics in the modern era is actually the outplaying of a much lengthier process that has long dominated the history of Christianity in the West and its complex involvements within the political sphere. What we in the West have often taken to be exclusively a theological or doctrinal development has typically contained at its heart a political proposition that can only be said to exist, and certainly has been disseminated through, a particular theological language. Such was what Carl Schmitt saw, for example, as the real fruits of theological speculation. Borrowing from the writings of Søren Kierkegaard—a writer whose work inspired and continues to inspire countless Protestant theologies in the modern era—Schmitt highlighted the exceptional status that faith takes in a person's life as it can be translated into the secular and political domain as a "state of exception" that legitimates the sovereign's right to rule. That is, whatever autonomous sovereign power claims the right to rule and to establish law in its name does so on the bedrock of an illusion, as if nothing had existed prior to its rule and so nothing could challenge its violently established autonomy. The sovereign's ability to rule was based upon a state of exceptionality that was created *ex nihilo*, miraculously as it were.[9]

What Schmitt detected in Kierkegaard's thought was nothing short of the ultimate grounds for political justification. Schmitt even went so far as to detect how the theological concept of the miracle was in truth the clearest expression of what political exceptionalism entailed—the sovereign could suspend the normal state of affairs just as God declares God's own sovereignty through the extension of a miraculous intervention which too suspends the normal laws of our universe or of physics in general. The decision of the sovereign was the foundation from which sovereignty itself sprung. The simple act of making the decision, of being the sole person who could decide in absolute freedom, was in fact what established the sovereign *as* sovereign. Schmitt's detection of a political-theological nexus at the center of Western thought is moreover what enables the critical eye to discern in many Christian believers, for example, deeply political motives within the apparently "politically neutral" acts of belief and conversion, which are really acts undertaken in order to establish the self as sovereign over itself in some sense (and though this is not, of course, all that such acts of belief do). This dynamic was in many ways what motivated the Lutheran challenge to the Catholic Church's hierarchy as well as the establishment of modern subjectivity, and the reason why, even and especially today, the fervent desire of the (often evangelical) Christian to make a "decision for Christ" is categorically about establishing one's individual sense of self in a way that cannot be challenged or contested. Hence, one can perceive overt gestures of sovereignty within the tautological apologetics one frequently encounters when questioning why and how a particular believer believes, often meeting such responses as "I know because I know because I know" or "you don't have to understand or agree, but I know I have a solid foundation upon which to stand. I know where my salvation lies," and so forth.

When perceived from this angle, the entire edifice of religious belief in the modern period, especially in its various Christian and even evangelical forms, becomes revealed as a political-theological experiment in constructing subjects who are fully confident of their foundations in themselves through what amounts to the fiction of faith itself (akin to the fiction of sovereignty, as in Hans Christian Andersen's "The Emperor's New Clothes"). It is in this exact sense that we begin to see anew the ever-present issue of theodicy, which begs the question of why a good God does not intervene in our world when so much suffering exists. Theodicy, in this context, can be understood not primarily as a radical challenge to God's existence, but rather as housing a laboratory for the apparent legitimations of authority.[10] That is, the question of theodicy is really a question concerning who has the right to rule: God *or* the powers of individual or collective persons? The question of theodicy as such reveals the intensely political nature of suffering in the modern era and the legitimacy of sovereign power alongside it. It is relatively easy to see from these developments that so many attempts to prove the existence of God—including Christian appropriations of Aristotle's argument of the "unmoved mover," for example—are really little more than attempts to legitimate the existence of a particular sovereign power, or, in the modern era, of the state.[11]

It is not only certain figures in modernity, however, that have been intensely invested in discerning the political stakes of various theological questions. That is to say, the various theological issues that appear to us in the modern period as having been secularized are really demonstrations of more fundamentally human issues that are neither fully religious nor fully secular—they are perhaps rather part of the "secularreligious," as Catherine Keller has put it.[12] They are conditions of living as a human being that defy such a dualistic categorization.

Such issues have plagued theological conversations from their inception, and they will continue to unsettle humanity in whatever new form they take. The history of debates on the Incarnation of Christ and ecclesial councils on the two natures of Jesus—human and divine—has often been, in reality, a political discussion on the question of authority, pitting those who would support monarchical rule (those arguing for Christ's divinity) against those who would challenge the King's political authority (those arguing for Jesus' humanity).[13] The bifurcated nature of Jesus was what had even defined the dominant model of medieval political theology, the King's two bodies, as Ernst Kantorowicz has already illustrated.[14] It also gave rise to the supremacy of the "binity" in Western political thought that which displaced the trinity through its dependence upon politically dualistic schemata, as Roberto Esposito had demonstrated.[15]

All of these examples are to suggest that if theology has a future in the Western, modern world in which many of us live, it is either going to have to argue more vehemently than ever before for its relevance while also avoiding the perils and pitfalls of trying to posit itself as a sovereign discourse among many other competing claims, *or* going to have to learn to articulate its core truth—the relationship between truth, poverty, and existence that I have been arguing for throughout—more clearly than ever, though also weakening itself in the process.

Whither Theology?

Theological history is besieged with defenses of God's sovereignty as the basis for those metaphysical propositions that theologians and ecclesial masters have been more than willing to defend. Various tomes have expanded throughout the centuries on the nature of the divine as bound up with necessity and providence, as a "Pure Act," as the highest thought which could be thought, as the ultimate sovereign power, and as the sole legitimate instigator of just violence in our world. As each of these claims has been made, we have witnessed at the same time passionate theological counter-defenses that have argued for contingency and free will, the endless potentiality of divine substance, the poverty of thought and of being, rendering inoperative the power of sovereignty and the impossibility and injustice of violent actions. Though the latter forces have paraded throughout history under a variety of names—generally, those resonant with radical revolutionaries, heresy, unorthodox views, and antinomian sentiments—there is a truth to such positions that we can no longer afford to ignore or suppress as if they were simply errant claims made to assault the bastions of theological integrity. The assault, in so many words, has come rather from *within* the fortress, not exclusively from the outside.

Seeing things this way means not only learning how proofs for God's existence are, in reality, attempts to legitimate sovereign power, for example, but also in discerning how many contemporary trends in philosophical thought, such as aesthetic theories on the sublime, the excessive nature of the hyperbolic, and even nihilism itself are not irrelevant to theological claims. They are perhaps the new cornerstones upon which the future of theology is already being constructed. As Ray Brassier provocatively helps us to see, "Nihilism is not an existential quandary but a speculative opportunity."[16] If nihilism is to have meaning for the various threads I have been outlining throughout this short study then they are to be found within the possibility for a minimal theology to illuminate the various singularities and forms of life that humanity, as a whole, is called to respect. In such a fashion, meaning is to be found even in an apparent postmodern nihilism that presents itself as the opposing force to any authoritarian or ideological tendencies in the West.[17] By suggesting this, I share with those readings of postmodernity that would see nihilism and the sublime not as opposed to each other, but as forces working toward a common goal.[18]

Though theology has, recently and for centuries, demonstrated a strong opposition to anything that appeared as nihilistic, there are other trends at work today that would point toward something like John Caputo's "nihilism of grace" in order to see how it possibly offers theological thought a chance for any future at all.[19] To see things this way, however, means learning to recognize as well how nihilism might be seen as an opportunity for clearing the ground for something better to come, not necessarily as suggesting what that something better must be. In this sense it most certainly will appear on occasion as an antinomian sensibility—something which queer theology, for one, has lately attempted to embody—in that it provides us with only a negative political theology and something like a negative ecclesiology that leaves many working within a theological context wondering what sort of concrete, practical future theology might have at all once all this deconstructive work has been carried out.[20]

To be fair, however, one must note too how theology has not been entirely averse to welcoming deconstructive activity throughout its long history. The vast realms of negative theology and of mystical insight—what has frequently been taken as representative of the "darkness of God"—speak to the conditions of nihilism and of a dialectics at a standstill, and such realms have often faced charges of heresy as a result. One might think here as well of various Trinitarian approaches to negativity insofar as the Spirit functions as a sign of the unending tension between the seemingly static God and the messianic Son who permanently undoes our representations of "the Father," invoking the sphere of absence as a creative principle which must constantly be rethought anew. The role of negativity in modern thought, from Hegel to Adorno to Žižek, is no less representative of such tensions and contentions, though it is no less illuminating either.

There is no doubt that the two sides of political theology, the positive and negative, must co-exist, much as *kataphatic* and *apophatic* theologies have co-existed, albeit uneasily at times, in a permanent tension or state of contradiction. Mining the depths of the political impulses within this tension as much as the theological implications of having such a tension in the first place is no doubt in order. Nevertheless it is at least clear at this moment in time that rather short shrift has been given to the negative side of things. This is a trend that is long in need of correction within the theological world.

In addition to such thoughts, within the modern era at least, political theology has become increasingly aware that the Church actually created the secular sphere through its designation of papal sovereignty as distinct from kingship.[21] To what degree atheism has also been created in modern form by (an initially Protestant) faith's retraction into the sphere of personal belief, leaving a general, secular, and potentially atheistic domain external to it, remains to be cemented in the popular imagination, though such a connection seems by now to be taking firm hold. To conceive of atheism in modernity alongside the philosophical giants of a Jean-Paul Sartre or a Jean-Luc Nancy means learning to think secularization in league with figures like Caputo and those championing the death of God as a possible opening to something like a divine presence in other, immanent forms. Or perhaps it means learning to read secularization itself as a movement of the divine in other guises, or simply as the logical conclusion to the Christian tradition's self-reflexive impetus. In this fashion, a sort of mystical reapproachment with modern secularism seems not only worth inspecting—it seems to be perhaps the best path forward for whatever minimal theology we place under immediate consideration.

The Idiocy of Theology

In his three-volume *Spheres* project, Peter Sloterdijk contemplates the contrast between the hierarchical angel as messenger of a traditional metaphysical paradigm, as well as the transcendent contents of its message, and the egalitarian idiot who speaks "never with authority, only with the force of his openness."[22] There is as such no content to their message. There is rather merely the "transforming intensity" that their presence brings with them, a "closeness in which contoured subjects can dissolve their boundaries and remold themselves."[23] Echoing Agamben's emphasis upon the weak messianic force as being that which carries no content, but only the power to divide every established social division, Sloterdijk points toward the figure of Jesus as an idiotic existence capable of producing transformative encounters without the need to justify his authority through a transcendent source. In such a way as this, we are given insight into just how an "intimacy without relations," as Agamben will call it, might be possible as an alternative route for theological propositions about the human world.[24]

If one of the most common criticisms of religious truth is that the sheer variety of competing religious truth claims is enough to render the casual observer not just skeptical, but forthrightly dismissive of religious doctrines, then it is indeed time to begin a comparative assessment of truths among religious traditions (and of certain marginalized traditions *within* specific religious traditions) that attempts to provide a source of self-critique.[25] As Jean-François Lyotard had pointed out in his book *The Differend*, there is a crucial difference between a grand narrative posing as absolute and one that undermines its own claims to totalization, while also presenting a universal position—a tendency he noted as present within the Christian tradition specifically.[26] It is time that Christianity, among other faiths within our world, acknowledges the profound transformations possible *for itself*, and only then for others, always however within the context of embracing its own poverty.

What if the messianic and highly *kenotic* trajectory embedded within the Christian tradition were an exemplary model for our present secular world, but only insofar as such claims were not the foundations for a resurgent Christendom, but rather insofar as they signaled the willingness of a religious tradition to empty itself of its own claims to power and privilege? What if Christianity poured itself out to the point of welcoming the absence of transcendence in our world and its accompanying metaphysics as its own narrative? What if, as the intellectual historian Larry Siedentop has pointed out, Christianity paves the way for its own demise, giving way to the secularism that it bequeathed to the West (and the world as a whole eventually) so that its messianic promise of an absolute *kenosis* might be fulfilled? Though this truly *minima theologica* might be more resonant with those "death of God" theologies than many Christians might be comfortable with, as well as with those who have signaled the importance of noting primarily the failure of Western theology as Marika Rose has recently done, there would nonetheless be a refusal to absolutize the values of one tradition over another that may also open a conversation between parties without the aggression, violence, dominance, oppression, and presumption that have characterized a good many religious conflicts over the centuries.[27]

Within this framework, Adorno's inverse theology is revealed as truly a weak theology and as an absolutely kenotic theology that concludes with the poverty of theology as Christianity's eventual dissolution in traditional religious form. Rather than this particular religion's demise being something to be avoided, however, what if it were accelerated and performed with the utmost care and attention toward the betterment of an intimacy between persons and groups that went beyond all defined relations and representations, as well as with the full acknowledgment of Christianity's role and story in such a process? Such a movement would certainly appear to many to be idiotic, as Sloterdijk has put it, or as a foolishness in the face of the world that would attract little more than ridicule and scorn, perhaps even from professional theologians or Church officials. But, on the other hand, could such an acceptance, perhaps even an obedience, also be a foolishness that Paul himself had foreseen as a novel font of wisdom in disguise (1 Corinthians 1:20-21)?

NOTES

Introduction

1 Mark Lewis Taylor, *The Theological and the Political: On the Weight of the World* (Minneapolis, MN: Fortress, 2011).

Chapter 1

1 Tomáš Halík, *Night of the Confessor: Christian Faith in an Age of Uncertainty* (New York: Image, 2012), p. 9.

2 Halík, *Night of the Confessor*, p. 211.

3 Halík, *Night of the Confessor*, p. 209. We might note how these conclusions are active in (a theological reading of) the work of Bruno Latour, for example, where the subject-object dichotomy is removed in favor of the multiplicity that emanates from objects themselves. See Adam Miller, *Speculative Grace: Bruno Latour and Object-Oriented Theology* (New York: Fordham University Press, 2013).

4 Pseudo-Dionysius, *The Complete Works*, ed. Colm Luibhéid, trans. Paul Rorem (Mahwah, NJ: Paulist Press, 1987). His endorsement of apophatic thought has also been read in opposition to the defense of ecclesial hierarchies, a point well worth contemplating. See David Newheiser, *Hope in a Secular Age: Deconstruction, Negative Theology, and the Future of Faith* (Cambridge: Cambridge University Press, 2019), pp. 139–40.

5 Jean-Luc Marion, *Negative Certainties*, trans. Stephen E. Lewis (Chicago: University of Chicago Press, 2015), p. 207.

6 Theodor W. Adorno, *Negative Dialectics*, trans. E. B. Ashton (London: Continuum, 1973), p. 12.

7 Theodor W. Adorno, *Against Epistemology: A Metacritique: Studies in Husserl and the Phenomenological Antinomies*, trans. Willis Domingo (Cambridge: Polity, 1982), p. 188.

8 See Jean-Luc Marion, *In Excess: Studies of Saturated Phenomena*, trans. Robyn Horner and Vincent Berraud (New York: Fordham University Press, 2004).

9 John D. Caputo, *How to Read Kierkegaard* (New York: W. W. Norton, 2008), p. 52.

10 Slavoj Žižek and John Milbank, *The Monstrosity of Christ: Paradox or Dialectic?* ed. Creston Davis (Cambridge, MA: MIT Press, 2009).

11 Tomáš Halík, *Patience with God: The Story of Zacchaeus Continuing in Us* (New York: Doubleday, 2009), p. 21.

12 Halík, *Patience with God*, p. 17, de-emphasized from the original. I do not think, in this sense, that secularization need be read as a gift from God in that it was an intentional or inevitable outcome of history, but rather that, if such a phenomenon can be understood to resonate with the deepest experiences of the spiritual life (e.g., the dark night of the soul, the atheism *within* the believer, etc.) then perhaps it can be read as containing a previously unforeseen gift that it will be humanity's job to remain open toward and so precisely to see as a most unexpected gift no matter if it is declared sacred or secular. Perhaps the true gift undoes the division itself.

13 Jacques Derrida, "*Sauf le nom (Post-Scriptum)*" *On the Name*, ed. Thomas Dutoit, trans. David Wood (Stanford: Stanford University Press, 1995), p. 35.

14 Derrida, "*Sauf le nom*," p. 54. See also John D. Caputo, *The Prayers and Tears of Jacques Derrida: Religion without Religion* (Bloomington: Indiana University Press, 1997), p. 2.

15 Derrida, "*Sauf le nom*," pp. 43, 59.

16 Jacques Derrida, "Envoi," in *Psyche: Inventions of the Other*, vol. 1, ed. Peggy Kamuf and Elizabeth Rottenberg, trans. Peter Caws and Mary Ann Caws (Stanford: Stanford University Press, 2007), as well as his *Aporias*, trans. Thomas Dutoit (Stanford: Stanford University Press, 1993), p. 16.

17 Derrida, "*Sauf le nom*," p. 36.

18 Derrida, "*Sauf le nom*," pp. 37–9, 48.

19 Derrida, "*Sauf le nom*," p. 40.

20 Derrida, "*Sauf le nom*," p. 42.

21 Derrida, "*Sauf le nom*," pp. 43, 50.

22 Derrida, "*Sauf le nom*," p. 50.

23 Derrida, "*Sauf le nom*," pp. 50–1.

24 Derrida, "*Sauf le nom*," p. 55.

25 Derrida, "*Sauf le nom*," pp. 55–6.

26 Derrida, "*Sauf le nom*," p. 67.

27 Derrida, "*Sauf le nom*," p. 79.

28 As the philosopher Giorgio Agamben has already noted in his work, the issue of possession is precisely what once made (and still makes) the Franciscan renunciation

of possessions so controversial within the history of the Catholic Church, an institution apparently very content at times to possess a good many things. Agamben, *The Highest Poverty: Monastic Rules and Form-of-Life*, trans. Adam Kostko (Stanford: Stanford University Press, 2013); see also the way in which Peter Fenves comments on Walter Benjamin's discussion of possession versus use in *The Messianic Reduction: Walter Benjamin and the Shape of Time* (Stanford: Stanford University Press, 2010), p. 189.

29 Carl Schmitt, *The Concept of the Political*, trans. George Schwab (Chicago: University of Chicago Press, 2007) and Gil Anidjar, *The Jew, the Arab: A History of the Enemy* (Stanford: Stanford University Press, 2003).

30 Caputo, *The Prayers and Tears of Jacques Derrida*, p. 2.

31 Paul Ricoeur, *On Translation*, trans. Eileen Brennan (Abingdon: Routledge, 2006), p. 32.

32 Adorno, *Negative Dialectics*, p. 375.

33 René Girard, *Things Hidden since the Foundation of the World*, trans. Stephen Bann and Michael Metteer (Stanford: Stanford University Press, 1987), p. 426.

34 Adorno, *Negative Dialectics*, p. 141.

35 See Gillian Rose, *The Melancholy Science: An Introduction to the Thought of Theodor W. Adorno* (London: Verso, 2014), p. 57.

36 Adorno, *Negative Dialectics*, p. 406. And, he continues, "Without a thesis of identity, dialectics is not the whole; but neither will it be a cardinal sin to depart from it in a dialectical step."

37 Adorno, *Negative Dialectics*, p. 129.

38 Giorgio Agamben, *The Time That Remains: A Commentary on the Letter to the Romans*, trans. Patricia Dailey (Stanford: Stanford University Press, 2005).

39 The standard version of such "paradoxical" harmonies resides in those religious beliefs wherein good and evil are both to be found, in perfect balance, in the divine being, like a cosmic yin and yang.

40 Adorno, *Negative Dialectics*, p. 407.

41 Carl Schmitt, *Political Theology: Four Chapters on the Concept of Sovereignty*, trans. George Schwab (Chicago: University of Chicago Press, 2005), p. 15.

42 Schmitt, *Political Theology*, p. 36.

43 Schmitt, *Political Theology*, p. 7.

44 Giorgio Agamben, *State of Exception: Homo Sacer II, 1*, trans. Kevin Attell (Chicago: University of Chicago Press, 2005), p. 86.

45 See Agamben, "Bartleby, or on Contingency," in *Potentialities: Collected Essays in Philosophy*, trans. Daniel Heller-Roazen (Stanford: Stanford University Press, 2000), pp. 243–73.

46 Agamben, *State of Exception*, p. 88. See also Giorgio Agamben, *Profanations*, trans. Jeff Fort (New York: Zone, 2007).

47 Žižek and Milbank, *The Monstrosity of Christ*, p. 87.

48 Søren Kierkegaard, *Fear and Trembling/Repetition*, trans. Edna H. Hong and Howard V. Hong (Princeton: Princeton University Press, 1983), pp. 54–7.

49 Søren Kierkegaard, *Concluding Unscientific Postscript to* Philosophical Fragments, vol. 1, trans. Edna H. Hong and Howard V. Hong (Princeton: Princeton University Press, 1992), pp. 204, 343. See also Søren Kierkegaard, *Practice in Christianity*, trans. Edna H. Hong and Howard V. Hong (Princeton: Princeton University Press, 1991), pp. 25, 82.

50 Kierkegaard, *Concluding Unscientific Postscript to* Philosophical Fragments, pp. 209–11.

51 Kierkegaard, *Concluding Unscientific Postscript to* Philosophical Fragments, pp. 318–41.

52 Gary Dorrien, *The Barthian Revolt in Modern Theology: Theology without Weapons* (Louisville, KY: Westminster John Knox Press, 1999).

53 Hans Urs von Balthasar, *The Theology of Karl Barth*, trans. Edward T. Oakes (San Francisco: Ignatius Press, 1992), pp. 107–67.

54 See Judith Butler, *Senses of the Subject* (New York: Fordham University Press, 2015), p. 140.

55 John Milbank, "Materialism and Transcendence," in *Theology and the Political: The New Debate*, ed. Creston Davis, John Milbank, and Slavoj Žižek (Durham, NC: Duke University Press, 2005), pp. 393–426.

56 Kierkegaard, *Concluding Unscientific Postscript to* Philosophical Fragments, pp. 431–2.

57 See Perry D, LeFevre's comments on such "Relative Ends," in Søren Kierkegaard, *The Prayers of Kierkegaard*, ed. Perry D. LeFevre (Chicago: University of Chicago, 1996), p. 179.

58 See Jürgen Moltmann, *The Crucified God: The Cross of Christ as the Foundations and Criticism of Christian Theology*, trans. R. A. Wilson and John Bowden (Minneapolis, MN: Fortress, 1993), p. 254, and Rubem A. Alves, *A Theology of Human Hope* (Washington, DC: Corpus Books, 1969), pp. 114–22.

59 Schmitt's influence on Benjamin's thought is perhaps most clearly noted in the latter's *The Origins of German Tragic Drama*, trans. John Osborne (London: Verso,

60 Walter Benjamin, "On the Concept of History," in *Selected Writings, Vol. 4, 1938–1940*, ed. Howard Eiland and Michael W. Jennings, trans. Harry Zohn (Cambridge, MA: Belknap, 1996), p. 390.

61 Walter Benjamin, *The Arcades Project*, trans. Howard Eiland and Kevin McLaughlin (Cambridge, MA: Belknap, 2002), p. 463.

62 Derrida, "*Sauf le nom*," p. 71.

63 Giorgio Agamben, *The Church and the Kingdom*, trans. Leland de la Durantaye (New York: Seagull, 2012), pp. 34–5.

64 Johann Baptist Metz, *Faith in History and Society: Toward a Practical Fundamental Theology*, trans. J. Matthew Ashley (New York: Crossroad, 2007), pp. 156–8. See also Lieven Boeve, *God Interrupts History: Theology in a Time of Upheaval* (London: Continuum, 2007).

65 Slavoj Žižek, *Less than Nothing: Hegel and the Shadow of Dialectical Materialism* (London: Verso, 2012), p. 294.

66 G. W. F. Hegel, *Science of Logic*, trans. A. V. Miller (Amherst, NY: Humanity, 1969), p. 834. Frederic Jameson makes essentially this same defense of Hegelian mediation between two poles as the authentic dialectic in his *Valences of the Dialectic* (London: Verso, 2009).

67 Žižek, *Less than Nothing*, p. 298. See also Žižek and Milbank, *The Monstrosity of Christ*, p. 70.

68 Žižek, *Less than Nothing*, p. 299. On Kierkegaard's Hegelianism, see Butler's chapter on Kierkegaard in her *Senses of the Subject*.

69 Agamben, *The Time That Remains*, pp. 47–9.

70 Agamben, *The Time That Remains*, p. 50.

71 Žižek and Milbank, *The Monstrosity of Christ*, p. 55.

72 Slavoj Žižek, *Absolute Recoil: Towards a New Foundation of Dialectical Materialism* (London: Verso, 2014), p. 337.

73 Žižek, *Absolute Recoil*, p. 337.

74 See Žižek, *Absolute Recoil*, p. 343.

75 Jean-Luc Nancy, *Dis-Enclosure: The Deconstruction of Christianity*, trans. Bettina Bergo, Gabriel Malenfant, and Michael B. Smith (New York: Fordham University Press, 2008).

76 Marcel Gauchet, *The Disenchantment of the World: A Political History of Religion*, trans. Oscar Burge (Princeton: Princeton University Press, 1997), pp. 61–2.

77 Žižek and Milbank, *The Monstrosity of Christ*, p. 59.

78 Žižek, *Less than Nothing*, p. 303.

79 Žižek, *Less than Nothing*, p. 303.

80 On the significance of failure within the context of Christian theological claims, see a work brought to contemporary attention through the efforts of Pope Francis, John Navone, *Triumph through Failure: A Theology of the Cross* (Homebush: St Paul, 1984).

81 Žižek, *Absolute Recoil*, p. 330.

82 Žižek, *Less than Nothing*, p. 981.

83 Žižek, *Absolute Recoil*, p. 81.

84 Žižek, *Absolute Recoil*, p. 344.

85 Žižek and Milbank, *The Monstrosity of Christ*, p. 71.

86 Žižek and Milbank, *The Monstrosity of Christ*, p. 101. This is what will allow Žižek to state, later on, that a thoroughly materialist theology is "[…] anything but boring. It is, on the contrary, breathtakingly surprising and paradoxical" (p. 240).

87 Žižek and Milbank, *The Monstrosity of Christ*, p. 298.

88 Žižek, *Absolute Recoil*, p. 349.

89 Žižek and Milbank, *The Monstrosity of Christ*, p. 248.

90 Žižek and Milbank, *The Monstrosity of Christ*, p. 253. Cf. his further remarks on paradox in Kierkegaard's work in Žižek and Milbank, *The Monstrosity of Christ*, p. 258.

91 I elaborate on these themes in greater depth in my *The Fetish of Theology: The Challenge of the Fetish-Object to Modernity* (London: Palgrave Macmillan, 2020).

92 Žižek and Milbank, *The Monstrosity of Christ*, p. 58.

93 Žižek, *Less than Nothing*, p. 987.

Chapter 2

1 On the general demise of grand narratives, see Jean-François Lyotard, *The Postmodern Condition: A Report on Knowledge*, trans. Geoffrey Bennington and Brian Massumi (Minneapolis: University of Minnesota Press, 1984).

2 See Joeri Schrijvers, *Ontotheological Turnings? The Decentering of the Modern Subject in Recent French Phenomenology* (Albany, NY: SUNY Press, 2011).

3   Adorno, *Negative Dialectics*, p. 367.

4   Adorno, *Negative Dialectics*, p. 398.

5   Adorno, *Negative Dialectics*, p. 207.

6   Jürgen Moltmann, *Theology of Hope: On the Ground and the Implications of a Christian Eschatology*, trans. James W. Leitch (Minneapolis, MN: Fortress, 1967), p. 211.

7   Moltmann, *The Crucified God*.

8   Adorno, *Negative Dialectics*, p. 203.

9   Adorno, *Negative Dialectics*, p. 399. See also Patrice Haynes, *Immanent Transcendence: Reconfiguring Materialism in Continental Philosophy* (London: Bloomsbury, 2014).

10 Adorno, *Negative Dialectics*, p. 401.

11 Adorno, *Negative Dialectics*, pp. 401–2.

12 Žižek and Milbank, *The Monstrosity of Christ*, p. 298.

13 Jacques Derrida, "Circumfessions," in *Jacques Derrida*, ed. Geoffrey Bennington, trans. Geoffrey Bennington (Chicago: University of Chicago Press, 1999), p. 155.

14 Haynes, *Immanent Transcendence*, pp. 149–50.

15 Adorno, *Negative Dialectics*, p. 393.

16 Adorno, *Negative Dialectics*, p. 406.

17 Adorno, *Negative Dialectics*, p. 408.

18 See Elliot R. Wolfson, *Open Secret: Postmessianic Messianism and the Mystical Revision of Menahem Mendel Schneerson* (New York: Columbia University Press, 2009), p. 182.

19 Adorno, *Negative Dialectics*, p. 408.

20 Adorno, *Negative Dialectics*, p. 181.

21 Adorno, *Negative Dialectics*, p. 182.

22 Adorno, *Negative Dialectics*, pp. 144, 28.

23 Adorno, *Negative Dialectics*, p. 365. See also Rosemary Radford Ruether, *The Church against Itself: An Inquiry into the Conditions of Historical Existence for the Eschatological Community* (New York: Herder & Herder, 1967).

24 Max Horkheimer and Theodor W. Adorno, *Dialectic of Enlightenment: Philosophical Fragments*, ed. Gunzelin Schmid Noerr, trans. Edmund Jephcott (Stanford: Stanford University Press, 2007), p. 8.

25 Horkheimer and Adorno, *Dialectic of Enlightenment*, pp. 11–12.

26 For more on a Girardian framework, see Scott Cowdell, *René Girard and Secular Modernity: Christ, Culture, and Crisis* (Notre Dame, IN: University of Notre Dame Press, 2013).

27 Moltmann, *Theology of Hope*, p. 171.

28 Adorno, *Negative Dialectics*, pp. 158, 148.

29 Agamben, *The Time That Remains*.

30 On the nature of the "whatever being," see Giorgio Agamben, *The Coming Community*, trans. Michael Hardt (Minneapolis: University of Minnesota Press, 1993); see also Colby Dickinson, *Agamben and Theology* (London: T&T Clark, 2011).

31 Adorno, *Negative Dialectics*, p. 118.

32 Maurice Blondel, *Action (1893): Essay on a Critique of Life and a Science of Practice*, trans. Oliva Blanchette (Notre Dame, IN: University of Notre Dame Press, 2004), pp. 285–99.

33 See also Bruno Latour, *On the Modern Cult of the Factish Gods* (Durham, NC: Duke University Press, 2010).

34 See, for instance, Emmanuel Falque, *The Metamorphosis of Finitude: An Essay on Birth and Resurrection*, trans. George Hughes (New York: Fordham University Press, 2012). Falque's work, in particular, runs parallel to much of what I am suggesting along these lines, including his focus on the subverting the Christian tradition from within through a phenomenological focus on both the fractures within finitude and the contours of human material embodiment. See also his account given in Emmanuel Falque, *The Wedding Feast of the Lamb: Eros, the Body, and the Eucharist*, trans. George Hughes (New York: Fordham University Press, 2016).

35 See, among others, Metz, *Faith in History and Society*.

36 Hent de Vries, *Minimal Theologies: Critiques of Secular Reason in Adorno and Levinas*, trans. Geoffrey Hale (Baltimore, MD: Johns Hopkins University Press, 2005) and Theodor W. Adorno, *Minima Moralia: Reflections on a Damaged Life*, trans. E. F. N. Jephcott (London: Verso, 2006).

37 de Vries, *Minimal Theologies*, p. 342.

38 Julia Kristeva, *This Incredible Need to Believe*, trans. Beverley Bie Brahic (New York: Columbia University Press, 2011), p. xv. It should come as no surprise too that Jean-Luc Nancy's account of the deconstruction of Christianity is compatible with his formulation of a "transcendence-in-immanence" that motivates his own wrestling with metaphysical speculation.

39 Kristeva, *This Incredible Need to Believe*, p. 70.

40 Kristeva, *This Incredible Need to Believe*, p. ix.

41 Julia Kristeva, *Hatred and Forgiveness*, trans. Jeanine Herman (New York: Columbia University Press, 2012), p. 210.

42 Kristeva, *Hatred and Forgiveness*, p. 210.

43 Kristeva, *This Incredible Need to Believe*, p. vii.

44 Kristeva, *This Incredible Need to Believe*, p. xv.

45 Kristeva, *This Incredible Need to Believe*, p. 3.

46 Kristeva, *This Incredible Need to Believe*, p. 7.

47 Kristeva, *This Incredible Need to Believe*, pp. 8, 54.

48 Kristeva, *This Incredible Need to Believe*, p. 12.

49 Kristeva, *Hatred and Forgiveness*, pp. 211–12.

50 Kristeva, *This Incredible Need to Believe*, p. 92.

51 Kristeva, *This Incredible Need to Believe*, p. 95.

52 Charles Taylor, *A Secular Age* (Cambridge, MA: Belknap, 2007), p. 772.

53 Taylor, *A Secular Age*, pp. 757–8.

54 Taylor, *A Secular Age*, p. 754.

55 Taylor, *A Secular Age*, p. 548.

56 Taylor, *A Secular Age*, pp. 531, 556.

57 Jean-Louis Chrétien, *The Unforgettable and the Unhoped For*, trans. Jeffrey Bloechl (New York: Fordham University Press, 2002).

58 Taylor, *A Secular Age*, p. 739.

59 Taylor, *A Secular Age*, p. 740.

60 Charles Taylor, "Preface," in *The Rivers North of the Future: The Testament of Ivan Illich as Told to David Cayley*, ed. Ivan Illich and David Cayley (Toronto: Anansi, 2005).

61 Taylor, *A Secular Age*, p. 743.

62 Taylor, *A Secular Age*, p. 743.

63 Taylor, *A Secular Age*, p. 712.

64 Ivan Illich and David Cayley, *The Rivers North of the Future*, p. 227.

65 Giorgio Agamben, *The Use of Bodies*, trans. Adam Kotsko (Stanford: Stanford University Press, 2016), pp. xx, 201.

66 Agamben, *The Use of Bodies*, pp. 201.

67 Giorgio Agamben, "In Praise of Profanation," in *Profanations*, p. 77.

68 Agamben, "In Praise of Profanation," p. 76.

69 Agamben, *The Use of Bodies*, pp. 72–3.

70 John Milbank, *Beyond Secular Order: The Representation of Being and the Representation of the People* (Oxford: Wiley-Blackwell, 2013), pp. 16, 257.

71 Milbank, *Beyond Secular Order*, p. 259.

72 Milbank, *Beyond Secular Order*, p. 259. The real influence behind all four thinkers would seem to be Michel Foucault, whose genealogical methods seem to dominate their chosen methodologies. Though Agamben is the only one to openly recognize Foucault's influence upon his work, the genealogical project lingers through them all.

73 Taylor, *A Secular Age*, pp. 90–145.

74 Though I will perhaps be enlightened by subsequent commentary on Agamben's work as offered by Milbank, his reading of Agamben's genealogical projects as concluding in the general direction of his own theological project needs much clarification in light of Agamben's own development of an "ontology of poverty."

75 Gerhart B. Ladner, *The Idea of Reform: Its Impact on Christian Thought and Action in the Age of the Fathers* (Cambridge, MA: Harvard University Press, 1959), pp. 436, 441.

76 Ladner, *The Idea of Reform*, p. 437.

77 See the conclusions reached in Giorgio Agamben, *The Church and the Kingdom*.

78 Michel de Certeau, *Culture in the Plural*, trans. Tom Conley (Minneapolis, MN: University of Minnesota Press, 1997), pp. 85–7.

79 Erich Fromm, "Disobedience as a Psychological and Moral Problem," in *Disobedience and Other Essays* (New York: Seabury, 1981), p. 17.

80 Ladner, *The Idea of Reform*, p. 35.

81 Ladner, *The Idea of Reform*, p. 35.

82 Ladner, *The Idea of Reform*, p. 35.

83 John Caputo, *The Weakness of God: A Theology of the Event* (Bloomington: Indiana University Press, 2006), p. 74.

84 Caputo, *The Weakness of God*, p. 93.

85 Caputo, *The Weakness of God*, pp. 102, 149.

86 Caputo, *The Weakness of God*, p. 151.

Chapter 3

1 John D. Caputo, *Hoping against Hope: Confessions of a Postmodern Pilgrim* (Minneapolis, MN: Fortress Press, 2015), pp. 173–4.

2   Stanley Rosen, *Nihilism: A Philosophical Essay* (New Haven, CT: Yale University Press, 1969), p. 140.

3   Slavoj Žižek, *The Sublime Object of Ideology* (London: Verso, 1989), p. 206.

4   Adorno, *Minima Moralia*, p. 226.

5   Adorno, *Minima Moralia*, p. 226.

6   Theodor W. Adorno, *Aesthetic Theory*, ed. and trans. Robert Hullot-Kentor (Minneapolis: University of Minnesota Press, 1998), p. 227.

7   Adorno, *Aesthetic Theory*, p. 227.

8   This tension is the same impulse that motivated, and motivates, the division between Protestantism (as spiritual) and Catholicism (as material), or that more originally between Christianity (as spiritual) and Judaism (as material). Humanity, at least in the West, is caught in a cycle of perpetual reformations and potential schisms with whatever institutional identity seems to grant it a foundational sense of self.

9   Immanuel Kant, *Critique of the Power of Judgment*, trans. Paul Guyer and Eric Matthews (Cambridge: Cambridge University Press, 2001), pp. 124–5.

10 Eli Friedlander, *Expressions of Judgment: An Essay on Kant's Aesthetics* (Cambridge, MA: Harvard University Press, 2015), p. 53.

11 Friedlander, *Expressions of Judgment*, p. 57.

12 In this it perhaps shares with John Keats's suggestion of a poetic "negative capability" that can be said to destroy our sense of the beautiful as the only means of actually preserving it, though in completely altered form (here as the sublime). For a productive theological engagement with the sublime, see Clayton Crockett, *A Theology of the Sublime* (London: Routledge, 2001). On the limits of the sublime see too Jean-Luc Nancy, "The Sublime Offering," in *A Finite Thinking*, ed. Simon Sparks, trans. Jeffrey Libbrett (Stanford: Stanford University Press, 2003), pp. 211–44.

13 Kant, *Critique of the Power of Judgment*, p. 125.

14 Kant, *Critique of the Power of Judgment*, p. 126.

15 Kant, *Critique of the Power of Judgment*, p. 186.

16 See Friedlander, *Expressions of Judgment*, pp. 74–5.

17 See Friedlander, *Expressions of Judgment*, p. 83.

18 Kant, *Critique of the Power of Judgment*, pp. 126–7.

19 Kant, *Critique of the Power of Judgment*, p. 126.

20 Kant, *Critique of the Power of Judgment*, p. 128.

21 Kant, *Critique of the Power of Judgment*, pp. 128–9.

22 Kant, *Critique of the Power of Judgment*, p. 129.

23 Kant, *Critique of the Power of Judgment*, pp. 138–9.

24 Kant, *Critique of the Power of Judgment*, p. 141.

25 Kant, *Critique of the Power of Judgment*, pp. 151–2.

26 Jean-François Lyotard, *Lessons on the Analytic of the Sublime*, trans. Elizabeth Rottenberg (Stanford: Stanford University Press, 1994). See also Gordon C. F. Bearn, *Life Drawing: A Deleuzean Aesthetics of Existence* (New York: Fordham University Press, 2013), p. 210.

27 See, among others, the commentary offered in Michael J. Shapiro, *The Political Sublime* (Durham, NC: Duke University Press, 2018).

28 Kant, *Critique of the Power of Judgment*, pp. 144–5.

29 Kant, *Critique of the Power of Judgment*, p. 146.

30 Kant, *Critique of the Power of Judgment*, pp. 160, 169.

31 Kant, *Critique of the Power of Judgment*, p. 167.

32 Kant, *Critique of the Power of Judgment*, p. 167.

33 Kant, *Critique of the Power of Judgment*, p. 168.

34 Kant, *Critique of the Power of Judgment*, pp. 214–17.

35 Kant, *Critique of the Power of Judgment*, p. 217.

36 Kant, *Critique of the Power of Judgment*, p. 217.

37 See how this argument is developed in Terry Eagleton, *Culture and the Death of God* (New Haven, CT: Yale University Press, 2014), p. 153.

38 Kant, *Critique of the Power of Judgment*, pp. 173–6.

39 *Fidei depositum*, for example, was the title of Pope John Paul II's apostolic constitution that decreed the publication of the Catechism of the Catholic Church.

40 Friedlander, *Expressions of Judgment*, p. 95.

41 Caputo, *Hoping against Hope*, p. 173.

42 Christoph Menke, *The Sovereignty of Art: Aesthetic Negativity in Adorno and Derrida*, trans. Neil Solomon (Cambridge, MA: MIT Press, 1998).

43 Hans-Georg Gadamer, *Truth and Method*, trans. Joel Weinsheimer and Donald G. Marshall (London: Continuum, 1975).

44 Sublime understanding, in Pillow's words, "always asserts the validity of the networked relations it finds or invents within contexts that both provide and limit the possibilities of discovery and fabrication." Kirk Pillow, *Sublime Understanding: Aesthetic Reflection in Kant and Hegel* (Cambridge, MA: MIT Press, 2000), pp. 316–17.

45 See, for example, Jacob Taubes, *The Political Theology of Saint Paul*, trans. Dana Hollander (Stanford: Stanford University Press, 2003), Alain Badiou, *Saint Paul: The Foundation of Universalism*, trans. Ray Brassier (Stanford: Stanford University Press, 2003), Slavoj Žižek, *The Ticklish Subject: The Absent Centre of Political Ontology* (London: Verso, 2000) and Agamben, *The Time That Remains*.

46 See the analysis and conclusions offered in Judith Butler, *The Psychic Life of Power: Theories in Subjection* (Stanford: Stanford University Press, 1997).

47 Žižek, *The Sublime Object of Ideology*.

48 Theodor W. Adorno, *The Jargon of Authenticity*, trans. Knut Tarnowski and Frederic Will (London: Routledge, 2003), p. xix.

49 I have pursued this theme in a related manner in "Slavoj Žižek on Jacques Derrida, or on Derrida's Search for a Middle Ground between Marx and Benjamin, and His Finding Žižek instead," *Philosophy Today* 59:2 (2015), pp. 291–304.

50 Eagleton, *Culture and the Death of God*, pp. 33, 39.

51 Eagleton, *Culture and the Death of God*, p. 39.

52 Eagleton, *Culture and the Death of God*, p. 35.

53 This rivalry is also what will allow Adorno to suggest that both art and religion find their roots in a more primordial fetishism. Agamben too will postulate an even more primordial relationship between religion and law, one that gives rise to the "magical" appearance of both insofar as they confront the limits of language, what he sees in the origin and nature of the oath. Cf. the attempt to replace religion with aesthetics in Herbert Marcuse, *The Aesthetic Dimension: Toward a Critique of Marxist Aesthetics*, trans. Erica Sherover (Boston: Beacon, 1979).

54 Eagleton, *Culture and the Death of God*, p. 174.

55 Eagleton, *Culture and the Death of God*, p. 49.

56 Eagleton, *Culture and the Death of God*, p. 114.

57 Eagleton, *Culture and the Death of God*, p. 115.

58 Eagleton, *Culture and the Death of God*, pp. 181–2.

59 Eagleton, *Culture and the Death of God*, p. 143.

60 Eagleton, *Culture and the Death of God*, p. 68.

61 See Eagleton, *Culture and the Death of God*, p. 136.

62 Taylor, *A Secular Age*, pp. 346–7.

63 Taylor, *A Secular Age*, p. 338.

64 See Hans Urs von Balthasar, *The Glory of the Lord: A Theological Aesthetics, Volume V: The Realm of Metaphysics in the Modern Age* (San Francisco: Ignatius Press, 2011), p. 484.

65 Von Balthasar, *The Glory of the Lord*, vol. 5, p. 483.

66 Von Balthasar, *The Glory of the Lord*, vol. 5, p. 493.

67 Von Balthasar, *The Glory of the Lord*, vol. 5, pp. 495–6.

68 Von Balthasar, *The Glory of the Lord*, vol. 5, p. 506, emphasis in the original.

69 Von Balthasar, *The Glory of the Lord*, vol. 5, p. 507.

70 See also Louis Roberts, *The Theological Aesthetics of Hans Urs von Balthasar* (Washington, DC: Catholic University of America Press, 1987), p. 212.

71 See Dorrien, *The Barthian Revolt in Modern Theology*.

72 We might think here of someone like Stanley Hauerwas, who combines many of these strands and whom Taylor cites as a complimentary theological viewpoint to his own. See Taylor, *A Secular Age*, p. 295.

73 See Giorgio Agamben, *The Kingdom and the Glory: For a Theological Genealogy of Economy and Government*, trans. Lorenzo Chiesa, with Matteo Mandarini (Stanford: Stanford University Press, 2011).

74 Johann Baptist Metz, *Poverty of Spirit*, trans. John Drury (Mahwah, NJ: Paulist Press, 1968), p. 25.

75 For more on the concept of stasis as a "political paradigm," see Giorgio Agamben, *Stasis: Civil War as a Political Paradigm*, trans. Nicholas Heron (Stanford: Stanford University Press, 2015).

76 Metz, *Poverty of Spirit*, p. 29.

77 Giorgio Agamben, *Homo Sacer: Sovereign Power and Bare Life*, trans. Daniel Heller-Roazen (Stanford: Stanford University Press, 1998).

78 Immanuel Kant, *Religion and Rational Theology*, trans. Allen W. Wood and George Di Giovanni (Cambridge: Cambridge University Press, 2001).

79 Metz, *Poverty of Spirit*, p. 30.

80 Metz, *Poverty of Spirit*, p. 38.

81 Metz, *Poverty of Spirit*, p. 46.

82 Metz, *Poverty of Spirit*, p. 47.

Chapter 4

1 Cf. Bruno Latour, *An Inquiry into Modes of Existence: An Anthropology of the Moderns*, trans. Catherine Porter (Cambridge, MA: Harvard University Press, 2013), pp. 168, 197.

2   Kant, *Critique of the Power of Judgment*, p. 146.

3   Judith Butler has more recently provided us with a series of insightful reflections on the relationship between violence and precarity, though I am taking up this discussion in a slightly nuanced fashion, asking questions specifically about memorialization and the sublime in relation to political points of origin. See Judith Butler, *Precarious Life: The Powers of Mourning and Violence* (London: Verso, 2004).

4   René Girard, *The Scapegoat*, trans. Yvonne Freccero (Baltimore, MD: Johns Hopkins University Press, 1989), p. 204.

5   René Girard, *I See Satan Fall Like Lightning*, trans. James G. Williams (Maryknoll, NY: Orbis, 2001), p. 92.

6   F. R. Ankersmit, *Sublime Historical Experience* (Stanford: Stanford University Press, 2005), pp. 336–7.

7   "The historical sublime is also a liminal phenomenon demarcating the phase of the subjective mind from that of the objective mind. And, as with myth, our crossing of this liminal threshold from the former to the latter is accompanied by a true storm of historicization or narrativization. History then becomes an almost tangible reality: One really feels that from now on one belongs to a different world and that a former part of ourselves has died off and become a lifeless and empty shell." Ankersmit, *Sublime Historical Experience*, p. 365.

8   Girard, *I See Satan Fall Like Lightning*, pp. 91–2. See too the pertinent remarks made concerning the non-existence of a tomb in the Gospel resurrection narratives in Gil Bailie, *Violence Unveiled: Humanity at the Crossroads* (New York: Crossroad, 1995), pp. 228–33.

9   Girard, *Things Hidden since the Foundation of the World*, p. 164.

10 Girard, *Things Hidden since the Foundation of the World*, p. 163.

11 Girard, *Things Hidden since the Foundation of the World*, p. 163.

12 Girard, *Things Hidden since the Foundation of the World*, p. 164.

13 Girard, *I See Satan Fall Like Lightning*, p. 86.

14 Paul Ricoeur, *Memory, History, Forgetting*, trans. Kathleen Blamey and David Pellauer (Chicago: University of Chicago Press, 2006), p. 82.

15 Ricoeur, *Memory, History, Forgetting*, p. 85.

16 Ricoeur, *Memory, History, Forgetting*, p. 85.

17 Paul Ricoeur, *Time and Narrative*, vol. 3, trans. Kathleen Blamey and David Pellauer (Chicago: University of Chicago Press, 1990), p. 237.

18 Ricoeur, *Time and Narrative*, vol. 3, p. 237.

19 See Ankersmit, *Sublime Historical Experience*, p. 321, as well as Ricoeur, *Memory, History, Forgetting*, p. 496.

20 Paul Ricoeur, *The Rule of Metaphor: The Creation of Meaning in Language*, trans. Robert Czerny with Kathleen McLaughlin and John Costello (London: Routledge, 1978), p. 371.

21 Žižek, *The Sublime Object of Ideology*.

22 Friedrich Nietzsche, *Untimely Meditations*, ed. Daniel Breazeale, trans. R. J. Hollingdale (Cambridge: Cambridge University Press, 1997) and Jean-François Lyotard, *The Differend: Phrases in Dispute*, trans. Georges Van Den Abbeele (Minneapolis: University of Minnesota Press, 1988).

23 Ricoeur, *The Rule of Metaphor*, pp. 322, 327.

24 Milbank, "Materialism and Transcendence," pp. 417–18.

25 See this formulation of in Adorno, *Negative Dialectics*.

26 David Tracy, *The Analogical Imagination: Christian Theology and the Culture of Pluralism* (New York: Crossroad, 1981), p. 421.

27 "For myself, the overwhelming reality disclosed in the originating event of Jesus Christ is none other than grace itself." Tracy, *The Analogical Imagination*, p. 430.

28 Miroslav Volf, *The End of Memory: Remembering Rightly in a Violent World* (Grand Rapids, MI: Eerdmans, 2006), p. 232.

29 Ricoeur, *Time and Narrative*, vol. 3, p. 238.

30 Ricoeur, *Time and Narrative*, vol. 3, p. 240.

31 See Jacques Derrida, "Force of Law," in *Acts of Religion*, ed. Gil Anidjar, trans. Mary Quaintance (London: Routledge, 2002).

32 Ricoeur, *Time and Narrative*, vol. 3, p. 240.

33 Paul Ricoeur, "The Memory of Suffering," in *Figuring the Sacred: Religion, Narrative and Imagination*, ed. Mark I. Wallace (Minneapolis, MN: Fortress Press, 1995), p. 290.

34 Gianni Vattimo, *Belief*, trans. Luca D'Isanto and David Webb (Stanford: Stanford University Press, 1999).

35 This is the basis of Slavoj Žižek's reading of Agamben, whose notion of profanation, Žižek argues, actually brings us, paradoxically, to the zero-level of the sacred. See Žižek, *Less than Nothing*, pp. 984–8.

36 See the arguments made in Robert A. Orsi, *History and Presence* (Cambridge, MA: Belknap Press, 2016), pp. 249–52.

37 Giorgio Agamben, *Nudities*, trans. David Kishik and Stefan Pedatella (Stanford: Stanford University Press, 2010), p. 90.

38 Agamben, *Profanations*.

39 Benjamin, "On the Concept of History," p. 391. On the conceptualization of a "dangerous memory," see Metz, *Faith in History and Society*.

40 Benjamin, "On the Concept of History," pp. 395–6.
41 Jean-Yves Lacoste, *Experience and the Absolute: Disputed Questions on the Humanity of Man*, trans. Mark Raftery-Skehan (New York: Fordham University Press, 2004).
42 See Jean-Luc Marion, *The Visible and the Revealed*, trans. Christina Gschwandtner (New York: Fordham University Press, 2008).
43 Richard Kearney, *Strangers, Gods and Monsters: Interpreting Otherness* (London: Routledge, 2005).
44 Richard Kearney, *The God Who May Be: A Hermeneutics of Religion* (Bloomington, IN: Indiana University Press, 2001).
45 See Jean-François Lyotard, *Lessons on the Analytic of the Sublime*.
46 Lyotard, *The Differend*.
47 Lyotard, *The Differend*, p. 165.
48 This insight is based on Carl Schmitt's division between sovereignty and liberalism in his *Political Theology*.
49 Ricoeur, *The Rule of Metaphor*, p. 291.
50 Ricoeur, *The Rule of Metaphor*, pp. 294, 300.
51 Ricoeur, *The Rule of Metaphor*, pp. 327–8, 340–1.
52 Ricoeur, *The Rule of Metaphor*, p. 363.
53 Giorgio Agamben, *State of Exception*.
54 Laurence Paul Hemming, *Postmodernity's Transcending: Devaluing God* (Notre Dame, IN: University of Notre Dame Press, 2005), p. 242.
55 Hemming, *Postmodernity's Transcending*, p. 231.
56 Hemming, *Postmodernity's Transcending*, p. 245.
57 Ricoeur, *The Rule of Metaphor*, p. 352.
58 Ricoeur, *The Rule of Metaphor*, p. 358.
59 Ricoeur, *The Rule of Metaphor*, p. 370.
60 Ricoeur, *The Rule of Metaphor*, p. 371.

Chapter 5

1 See Richard P. McBrien, *The Church: The Evolution of Catholicism* (New York: HarperOne, 2008), ch. 1.

2   See, among other instances of the use of revolutionary language within theological discourse, Diarmuid O'Murchu, *Christianity's Dangerous Memory: A Rediscovery of the Revolutionary Jesus* (New York: Crossroad, 2011). On the use of "dangerous memories" in a political-theological context, see Metz, *Faith in History and Society*.

3   H. Richard Niebuhr, *Christ and Culture* (New York: Harper & Row, 1951). See too subsequent critiques and commentary on Niebuhr's original typology in, among others, D. A. Carson, *Christ and Culture Revisited* (Grand Rapids, MI: Eerdmans, 2012).

4   See Marcel Gauchet's commentary on the ambiguity latent within Christianity's foundations in his *The Disenchantment of the World*, pp. 127–33.

5   This dualism is given by Fromm, *On Disobedience and Other Essays*.

6   See Michelle Voss Roberts, *Dualities: A Theology of Difference* (Louisville, KY: Westminster John Knox Press, 2010).

7   Walter Benjamin, "Critique of Violence," in *Selected Writings, Vol. 1, 1913–1926*, ed. Marcus Bullock and Michael W. Jennings, trans. Edmund Jephcott (Cambridge, MA: Belknap, 1996).

8   Giorgio Agamben, *State of Exception*.

9   Hannah Arendt, *On Violence* (New York: Harcourt, 1969), p. 43.

10 Arendt, *On Violence*, p. 42.

11 Arendt, *On Violence*, p. 30.

12 Arendt, *On Violence*, p. 48.

13 Arendt, *On Violence*, p. 49.

14 Arendt, *On Violence*, p. 52.

15 Arendt, *On Violence*, p. 53.

16 Arendt, *On Violence*, p. 79.

17 Arendt, *On Violence*, p. 80.

18 Insofar as it overlaps a good deal with Arendt's analysis of violence, we might also look to Judith Butler's articulation of nonviolence as what can only be accomplished through structural changes for greater forms of equality. See Judith Butler, *The Force of Non-Violence* (London: Verso, 2020).

19 Hannah Arendt, *On Revolution* (New York: Penguin, 1963), p. 16.

20 See G. W. F. Hegel, *Phenomenology of Spirit*, trans. A. V. Miller (Oxford: Oxford University Press, 1977).

21 See the commentary of Arendt's ambiguous use of absolutism in Samuel Moyn, "Hannah Arendt on the Secular," *New German Critique* 35:3 (2008), pp. 71–96.

22 Arendt, *On Revolution*, p. 16.

23 Benjamin, "Critique of Violence," p. 252. Giorgio Agamben, "On the Limits of Violence," trans. Elisabeth Fay, *diacritics* 39:4 (2009), pp. 103–11, p. 109. Originally published as "Sui limiti della violenza," *Nuovi argomenti* 17 (1970), pp. 159–73.

24 Giorgio Agamben, "The Idea of Language," in *Potentialities: Collected Essays in Philosophy*, trans. Daniel Heller-Roazen (Stanford: Stanford University Press, 1999), pp. 39–47.

25 Giorgio Agamben, "*Se: Hegel's Absolute and Heidegger's Erignis," in *Potentialities*, pp. 116–37.

26 It is of course intriguing that this search for an absolute position is precisely what Jacques Derrida had criticized in Agamben's work, suggesting that Agamben had continuously sought to be the author who would hold a position absolutely prior to any other one, hence his ability to be sovereign as author. See Jacques Derrida, *The Beast and the Sovereign, vol. 1*, ed. Michel Lisse, Marie-Louise Mallet, and Ginette Michaud, trans. Geoffrey Bennington (Chicago: University of Chicago Press, 2009), p. 92.

27 Jean-Paul Sartre, *Critique of Dialectical Reason*, vol. 2, trans. Quintin Hoare (London: Verso, 1991), p. 31.

28 Emmanuel Levinas, *Totality and Infinity: An Essay on Exteriority*, trans. Alphonso Lingis (Pittsburgh, PA: Duquesne University, 1969), p. 198.

29 Derrida, "Force of Law," p. 280.

30 Derrida, "Force of Law," p. 242.

31 The notion of self-sacrifice as a response to any claims of the violences of sovereignty, both theological and political, has been elaborated on in the work of the Czech philosopher Jan Patočka. See, in particular, the commentary offered on his notion of a kenotic sacrifice in chapter 7 of Martin Koči, *Thinking Faith after Christianity: A Theological Reading of Jan Patočka's Phenomenological Philosophy* (Albany: State University of New York Press, 2020).

32 Derrida, "Force of Law," p. 257.

33 See Jacques Derrida, *Specters of Marx: The State of the Debt, the Work of Mourning and the New International*, trans. Peggy Kamuf (London: Routledge, 1994).

34 Derrida, "Force of Law," p. 270.

35 Derrida, "Force of Law," pp. 272, 274.

36 See Jacques Derrida, "Canons and Metonymies," in *Logomachia: The Conflict of the Faculties Today*, ed. Richard Rand (Lincoln, NE: University of Nebraska Press, 1992).

37 Derrida, "Force of Law," p. 283.

38 Derrida, "Force of Law," p. 293.

39 Derrida, "Force of Law," p. 298.

40 Arendt, *On Revolution*, p. 25.

41 Arendt, *On Revolution*, p. 225.

42 See Agamben, *Homo Sacer*.

43 See Agamben, *The Highest Poverty*.

44 Agamben, "On the Limits of Violence," p. 107.

45 Benjamin, "Critique of Violence," p. 243.

46 As he would word the relationship of terms at the latest point in his life, "Thinking involves not only the movement of thoughts but their arrest as well. Where thinking suddenly comes to a stop in a constellation saturated with tensions, it gives that constellation a shock, by which thinking is crystallized as a monad. The historical materialist approaches a historical object only where it confronts him as a monad. In this structure he recognizes the sign of a messianic arrest of happening, or (to put it differently) a revolutionary chance in the fight for the oppressed past." Walter Benjamin, "On the Concept of History," p. 396.

47 Agamben, "On the Limits of Violence," p. 107.

48 Agamben, *Profanations*.

49 Slavoj Žižek, *Violence* (New York: Picador, 2008), p. 198.

50 Žižek, *Violence*, pp. 201, 205.

51 Žižek, *Violence*, p. 202. Cf. the critique of Žižek's reading of divine violence given in Mari Ruti, *The Singularity of Being: Lacan and the Immortal Within* (New York: Fordham University Press, 2012), pp. 108–10.

52 Agamben, *Profanations*, p. 77.

53 Agamben, *Profanations*, p. 79.

54 Agamben, *Profanations*, p. 81.

55 Žižek, *Less than Nothing*, p. 987.

56 Žižek, *Less than Nothing*, p. 988.

57 Dimitris Vardoulakis, *Sovereignty and Its Other: Toward the Dejustification of Violence* (New York: Fordham University Press, 2013), pp. 202–4.

58 See Žižek, *Less than Nothing*, pp. 975–81.

59 This is the conclusion drawn as well by Scott Cowdell in his *René Girard and Secular Modernity*, p. 179.

60 Girard, *I See Satan Fall Like Lightning*, p. 141.

61 See Girard, *I See Satan Fall Like Lightning*, pp. 192–3. See also 1 Corinthians 1:18-25.

62 Agamben, "On the Limits of Violence," p. 107.

63 Agamben, *The Time That Remains*.

64 Agamben, "On the Limits of Violence," p. 109.

65 Agamben, "On the Limits of Violence," p. 108.

66 Agamben, "On the Limits of Violence," p. 108.

67 Agamben, "On the Limits of Violence," p. 109.

68 Agamben, "On the Limits of Violence," p. 109.

69 Giorgio Agamben, "Creation and Salvation," in *Nudities*, p. 8.

70 Agamben, *The Use of Bodies*, pp. 266–9.

71 Agamben, *The Use of Bodies*, p. 269.

72 Agamben, *The Use of Bodies*, p. 273. Agamben cites in this context Paul's words from 1 Corinthians 15:24.

73 See Agamben, *The Time That Remains*, pp. 106–8.

74 Agamben, *The Use of Bodies*, p. 274.

75 Agamben, *The Use of Bodies*, p. 277.

76 See Agamben, *The Highest Poverty*.

Conclusion

1 Hans Blumenberg, *The Legitimacy of the Modern Age*, trans. Robert M. Wallace (Cambridge, MA: MIT Press, 1985), pp. 4–5.

2 Blumenberg, *The Legitimacy of the Modern Age*, pp. 14–15, 27.

3 Blumenberg, *The Legitimacy of the Modern Age*, p. 14.

4 Max Weber, *The Protestant Ethic and the Spirit of Capitalism, and Other Writings*, ed. and trans. Peter Baehr and Gordon C. Wells (New York: Penguin, 2002).

5 See Agamben, *The Kingdom and the Glory*.

6 See the arguments made in Webb Keane, *Christian Moderns: Freedom and Fetish in the Mission Encounter* (Berkeley, CA: University of California Press, 2007).

7 As Jean-Joseph Goux will elaborate on this state of things, "For the human subject is dispossessed of himself not only through his submission to the gods but, first and above all, through his reified relation to the state, to property, to commodities. The critique of God shifts to a critique of money and the state; theological criticism

becomes political criticism." Jean-Joseph Goux, *Symbolic Economies: After Marx and Freud*, trans. Jennifer Curtiss Gage (Ithaca, NY: Cornell University Press, 1990), pp. 153–4.

8   Goux, *Symbolic Economies*, p. 154.

9   This discussion takes place in Schmitt, *Political Theology*.

10 Adam Kotsko, *The Prince of This World* (Stanford, CA: Stanford University Press, 2016).

11 One might note here how Hobbes' definition of the Leviathan is analogous to Anselm's arguments on the existence of God. See Pierre Manent, *An Intellectual History of Liberalism*, trans. Rebecca Balinski (Princeton, NJ: Princeton University Press, 1996), pp. 20–38.

12 Catherine Keller, *Political Theology of the Earth: Our Planetary Emergency and the Struggle for a New Public* (New York: Columbia University Press, 2018), p. 18.

13 This is a recurring theme in Siedentop, *Inventing the Individual*.

14 Ernst Kantorowicz, *The King's Two Bodies: A Study in Medieval Political Theology* (Princeton, NJ: Princeton University Press, 2016).

15 Roberto Esposito, *Two: The Machine of Political Theology and the Place of Thought*, trans. Zakiya Hanafi (New York: Fordham University Press, 2015).

16 Ray Brassier, *Nihil Unbound: Enlightenment and Extinction* (London: Palgrave Macmillan, 2007), p. xi.

17 See the analysis of this "anti-authoritarian" nihilism in the conclusions of Shane Weller, *Modernism and Nihilism* (London: Palgrave Macmillan, 2011), p. 159.

18 See, in particular, Will Slocombe, *Nihilism and the Sublime Postmodern* (London: Routledge, 2005).

19 See, for example, the remarks on the overcoming of nihilism in Jean-Yves Lacoste, *From Theology to Theological Thinking*, trans. W. Chris Hackett (Charlottesville, VA: University of Virginia Press, 2014).

20 For more on what a possible "negative ecclesiology" might resemble, see my article "Exploring a Negative Catholic Ecclesiology in Conversation with Contemporary Continental Philosophy," *Ecclesia Semper Reformanda: Renewal and Reform beyond Polemics*, ed. Peter De Mey and Wim François (Leuven: Peeters, 2020), pp. 307–22.

21 See the general thesis explored in Larry Siedentop, *Inventing the Individual: The Origins of Western Liberalism* (Cambridge, MA: Belknap, 2014).

22 Peter Sloterdijk, *Spheres: Vol. 1: Bubbles: Microspherology*, trans. Wieland Hoban (South Pasadena, CA: Semiotext(e), 2011), p. 473.

23 Sloterdijk, *Spheres: Vol. 1*, p. 476.

24 Agamben, *The Use of Bodies*, p. 236.

25 See the critique offered in Philip Kitcher, *Life after Faith: The Case for Secular Humanism* (New Haven, CT: Yale University Press, 2014), pp. 3–15.

26 See Lyotard, *The Differend*, p. 159.

27 Marika Rose, *A Theology of Failure: Žižek against Christian Innocence* (New York: Fordham University Press, 2019).

BIBLIOGRAPHY

Adorno, Theodor W. *Aesthetic Theory*. Edited and translated by Robert Hullot-Kentor. Minneapolis: University of Minnesota Press, 1998.
Adorno, Theodor W. *Against Epistemology: A Metacritique: Studies in Husserl and the Phenomenological Antinomies*. Translated by Willis Domingo. Cambridge: Polity, 1982.
Adorno, Theodor W. *The Jargon of Authenticity*. Translated by Knut Tarnowski and Frederic Will. London: Routledge, 2003.
Adorno, Theodor W. *Minima Moralia: Reflections on a Damaged Life*. Translated by E. F. N. Jephcott. London: Verso, 2006.
Adorno, Theodor W. *Negative Dialectics*. Translated by E. B. Ashton. London: Continuum, 1973.
Agamben, Giorgio. *The Church and the Kingdom*. Translated by Leland de la Durantaye. New York: Seagull, 2012.
Agamben, Giorgio. *The Coming Community*. Translated by Michael Hardt. Minneapolis: University of Minnesota Press, 1993.
Agamben, Giorgio. *The Highest Poverty: Monastic Rules and Form-of-Life*. Translated by Adam Kotsko. Stanford: Stanford University Press, 2013.
Agamben, Giorgio. *Homo Sacer: Sovereign Power and Bare Life*. Translated by Daniel Heller-Roazen. Stanford: Stanford University Press, 1998.
Agamben, Giorgio. *The Kingdom and the Glory: For a Theological Genealogy of Economy and Government*. Translated by Lorenzo Chiesa, with Matteo Mandarini. Stanford: Stanford University Press, 2011.
Agamben, Giorgio. *Nudities*. Translated by David Kishik and Stefan Pedatella. Stanford: Stanford University Press, 2011.
Agamben, Giorgio. "On the Limits of Violence." Translated by Elisabeth Fay. *diacritics* 39:4 (2009), pp. 103–11. Originally published as Agamben, Giorgio. "Sui limiti della violenza." *Nuovi argomenti* 17 (1970), pp. 159–73.
Agamben, Giorgio. *Potentialities: Collected Essays in Philosophy*. Translated by Daniel Heller-Roazen. Stanford: Stanford University Press, 2000.
Agamben, Giorgio. *Profanations*. Translated by Jeff Fort. New York: Zone, 2007.
Agamben, Giorgio. *Stasis: Civil War as a Political Paradigm*. Translated by Nicholas Heron. Stanford: Stanford University Press, 2015.
Agamben, Giorgio. *State of Exception, Homo Sacer II*, 1. Translated by Kevin Attell. Chicago: University of Chicago Press, 2005.
Agamben, Giorgio. *The Time that Remains: A Commentary on the Letter to the Romans*. Translated by Patricia Dailey. Stanford: Stanford University Press, 2005.
Agamben, Giorgio. *The Use of Bodies*. Translated by Adam Kotsko. Stanford: Stanford University Press, 2016.

BIBLIOGRAPHY

Alves, Rubem A. *A Theology of Human Hope*. Washington, DC: Corpus Books, 1969.
Anidjar, Gil. *The Jew, the Arab: A History of the Enemy*. Stanford: Stanford University Press, 2003.
Ankersmit, F. R. *Sublime Historical Experience*. Stanford: Stanford University Press, 2005.
Arendt, Hannah. *On Revolution*. New York: Penguin, 1963.
Arendt, Hannah. *On Violence*. New York: Harcourt, 1969.
Badiou, Alain. *Saint Paul: The Foundation of Universalism*. Translated by Ray Brassier. Stanford: Stanford University Press, 2003.
Bailie, Gil. *Violence Unveiled: Humanity at the Crossroads*. New York: Crossroad, 1995.
Bearn, Gordon C. F. *Life Drawing: A Deleuzean Aesthetics of Existence*. New York: Fordham University Press, 2013.
Benjamin, Walter. *The Arcades Project*. Translated by Howard Eiland and Kevin McLaughlin. Cambridge, MA: Belknap, 2002.
Benjamin, Walter. *The Origins of German Tragic Drama*. Translated by John Osborne. London: Verso, 2009.
Benjamin, Walter. *Selected Writings, Vol. 4, 1938–1940*. Edited by Howard Eiland and Michael W. Jennings. Translated by Harry Zohn. Cambridge, MA: Belknap, 1996.
Benjamin, Walter. *Selected Writings, Vol. 1, 1913–1926*. Edited by Marcus Bullock and Michael W. Jennings. Translated by Edmund Jephcott. Cambridge, MA: Belknap, 1996.
Blondel, Maurice. *Action (1893): Essay on a Critique of Life and a Science of Practice*. Translated by Oliva Blanchette. Notre Dame, IN: University of Notre Dame Press, 2004.
Blumenberg, Hans. *The Legitimacy of the Modern Age*. Translated by Robert M. Wallace. Cambridge, MA: MIT Press, 1985.
Boeve, Lieven. *God Interrupts History: Theology in a Time of Upheaval*. London: Continuum, 2007.
Brassier, Ray. *Nihil Unbound: Enlightenment and Extinction*. London: Palgrave Macmillan, 2007.
Butler, Judith. *The Force of Non-Violence*. London: Verso, 2020.
Butler, Judith. *Precarious Life: The Powers of Mourning and Violence*. London: Verso, 2004.
Butler, Judith. *The Psychic Life of Power: Theories in Subjection*. Stanford: Stanford University Press, 1997.
Butler, Judith. *Senses of the Subject*. New York: Fordham University Press, 2015.
Caputo, John D. *Hoping against Hope: Confessions of a Postmodern Pilgrim*. Minneapolis, MN: Fortress Press, 2015.
Caputo, John D. *How to Read Kierkegaard*. New York: W. W. Norton, 2008.
Caputo, John D. *The Prayers and Tears of Jacques Derrida: Religion without Religion*. Bloomington: Indiana University Press, 1997.
Caputo, John D. *The Weakness of God: A Theology of the Event*. Bloomington: Indiana University Press, 2006.
Carson, D. A. *Christ and Culture Revisited*. Grand Rapids, MI: Eerdmans, 2012.
Chrétien, Jean-Louis. *The Unforgettable and the Unhoped For*. Translated by Jeffrey Bloechl. New York: Fordham University Press, 2002.
Cowdell, Scott. *René Girard and Secular Modernity: Christ, Culture, and Crisis*. Notre Dame, IN: University of Notre Dame Press, 2013.

Crockett, Clayton. *A Theology of the Sublime*. London: Routledge, 2001.
de Certeau, Michel. *Culture in the Plural*. Translated by Tom Conley. Minneapolis: University of Minnesota Press, 1997.
de Vries, Hent. *Minimal Theologies: Critiques of Secular Reason in Adorno and Levinas*. Translated by Geoffrey Hale. Baltimore, MD: Johns Hopkins University Press, 2005.
Derrida, Jacques. *Aporias*. Translated by Thomas Dutoit. Stanford: Stanford University Press, 1993.
Derrida, Jacques. *The Beast and the Sovereign, vol. 1*. Edited by Michel Lisse, Marie-Louise Mallet, and Ginette Michaud. Translated by Geoffrey Bennington. Chicago: University of Chicago Press, 2009.
Derrida, Jacques. "Canons and Metonymies." In *Logomachia: The Conflict of the Faculties Today*. Edited by Richard Rand. Lincoln, NE: University of Nebraska Press, 1992.
Derrida, Jacques. "Circumfessions." In *Jacques Derrida*. Edited by Geoffrey Bennington. Translated by Geoffrey Bennington. Chicago: University of Chicago Press, 1999.
Derrida, Jacques. "*Envoi*," *Psyche: Inventions of the Other*, vol. 1. Edited by Peggy Kamuf and Elizabeth Rottenberg. Translated by Stanford: Stanford University Press, 2007.
Derrida, Jacques. "Force of Law." In *Acts of Religion*. Edited by Gil Anidjar. Translated Mary Quaintance. London: Routledge, 2002.
Derrida, Jacques. "*Sauf le nom (Post-Scriptum),*" *On the Name*. Edited by Thomas Dutoit. Translated David Wood. Stanford: Stanford University Press, 1995.
Derrida, Jacques. *Specters of Marx: The State of the Debt, the Work of Mourning and the New International*. Translated by Peggy Kamuf. London: Routledge, 1994.
Dickinson, Colby. *Agamben and Theology*. London: T&T Clark, 2011.
Dickinson, Colby. "Exploring a Negative Catholic Ecclesiology in Conversation with Contemporary Continental Philosophy." In *Ecclesia Semper Reformanda: Renewal and Reform beyond Polemics*. Edited by Peter De Mey and Wim François. Leuven: Peeters, 2020, pp. 307–22.
Dickinson, Colby. "Slavoj Žižek on Jacques Derrida, or on Derrida's Search for a Middle Ground between Marx and Benjamin, and His Finding Žižek instead." *Philosophy Today* 59:2 (2015), pp. 291–304.
Dickinson, Colby. *The Fetish of Theology: The Challenge of the Fetish-Object to Modernity*. London: Palgrave Macmillan, 2020.
Dorrien, Gary. *The Barthian Revolt in Modern Theology: Theology without Weapons*. Louisville, KY: Westminster John Knox Press, 1999.
Eagleton, Terry. *Culture and the Death of God*. New Haven, CT: Yale University Press, 2014.
Eiland, Howard and Michael W. Jennings. *Walter Benjamin: A Critical Life*. Cambridge, MA: Belknap, 2014.
Esposito, Roberto. *Two: The Machine of Political Theology and the Place of Thought*. Translated by Zakiya Hanafi. New York: Fordham University Press, 2015.
Falque, Emmanuel. *The Metamorphosis of Finitude: An Essay on Birth and Resurrection*. Translated by George Hughes. New York: Fordham University Press, 2012.
Falque, Emmanuel. *The Wedding Feast of the Lamb: Eros, the Body, and the Eucharist*. Translated by George Hughes. New York: Fordham University Press, 2016.

Fenves, Peter. *The Messianic Reduction: Walter Benjamin and the Shape of Time*. Stanford: Stanford University Press, 2010.
Friedlander, Eli. *Expressions of Judgment: An Essay on Kant's Aesthetics*. Cambridge, MA: Harvard University Press, 2015.
Fromm, Erich. *On Disobedience and Other Essays*. New York: Seabury Press, 1981.
Gadamer, Hans-Georg. *Truth and Method*. Translated by Joel Weinsheimer and Donald G. Marshall. London: Continuum, 1975.
Gauchet, Marcel. *The Disenchantment of the World: A Political History of Religion*. Translated by Oscar Burge. Princeton, NJ: Princeton University Press, 1997.
Girard, René. *I See Satan Fall Like Lightning*. Translated by James G. Williams. Maryknoll, NY: Orbis, 2001.
Girard, René. *The Scapegoat*. Translated by Yvonne Freccero. Baltimore, MD: Johns Hopkins University Press, 1989.
Girard, René. *Things Hidden since the Foundation of the World*. Translated by Stephen Bann and Michael Metteer. Stanford: Stanford University Press, 1987.
Goux, Jean-Joseph. *Symbolic Economies: After Marx and Freud*. Translated by Jennifer Curtiss Gage. Ithaca, NY: Cornell University Press, 1990.
Halík, Tomáš. *Night of the Confessor: Christian Faith in an Age of Uncertainty*. New York: Image, 2012.
Halík, Tomáš. *Patience with God: The Story of Zacchaeus Continuing in Us*. New York: Doubleday, 2009.
Haynes, Patrice. *Immanent Transcendence: Reconfiguring Materialism in Continental Philosophy*. London: Bloomsbury, 2014.
Hegel, G. W. F. *Phenomenology of Spirit*. Translated by A. V. Miller. Oxford: Oxford University Press, 1977.
Hegel, G. W. F. *Science of Logic*. Translated by A. V. Miller. Amherst, NY: Humanity, 1969.
Hemming, Laurence Paul. *Postmodernity's Transcending: Devaluing God*. Notre Dame, IN: University of Notre Dame Press, 2005.
Horkheimer, Max and Theodor W. Adorno. *Dialectic of Enlightenment: Philosophical Fragments*. Edited by Gunzelin Schmid Noerr. Translated by Edmund Jephcott. Stanford: Stanford University Press, 2007.
Illich, Ivan and David Cayley. *The Rivers North of the Future: The Testament of Ivan Illich as Told to David Cayley*. Toronto: Anansi, 2005.
Jameson, Frederic. *Valences of the Dialectic*. London: Verso, 2009.
Kant, Immanuel. *Critique of Power of Judgment*. Edited by Paul Guyer. Translated by Paul Guyer and Eric Matthews. Cambridge: Cambridge University Press, 2000.
Kant, Immanuel. *Religion and Rational Theology*. Translated by Allen W. Wood and George Di Giovanni. Cambridge: Cambridge University Press, 2001.
Kantorowicz, Ernst. *The King's Two Bodies: A Study in Medieval Political Theology*. Princeton, NJ: Princeton University Press, 2016.
Keane, Webb. *Christian Moderns: Freedom and Fetish in the Mission Encounter*. Berkeley, CA: University of California Press, 2007.
Kearney, Richard. *The God Who May Be: A Hermeneutics of Religion*. Bloomington: Indiana University Press, 2001.

Kearney, Richard. *Strangers, Gods and Monsters: Interpreting Otherness*. London: Routledge, 2005.
Keller, Catherine. *Political Theology of the Earth: Our Planetary Emergency and the Struggle for a New Public*. New York: Columbia University Press, 2018.
Kierkegaard, Søren. *Concluding Unscientific Postscript to* Philosophical Fragments, vol. 1. Translated by Edna H. Hong and Howard V. Hong. Princeton: Princeton University Press, 1992.
Kierkegaard, Søren. *Fear and Trembling/Repetition*. Translated by Edna H. Hong and Howard V. Hong. Princeton: Princeton University Press, 1983.
Kierkegaard, Søren. *Practice in Christianity*. Translated by Edna H. Hong and Howard V. Hong. Princeton: Princeton University Press, 1991.
Kierkegaard, Søren. *The Prayers of Kierkegaard*. Edited by Perry D. LeFevre. Chicago: University of Chicago, 1996.
Kitcher, Philip. *Life after Faith: The Case for Secular Humanism*. New Haven, CT: Yale University Press, 2014.
Koči, Martin. *Thinking Faith after Christianity: A Theological Reading of Jan Patočka's Phenomenological Philosophy*. Albany: State University of New York Press, 2020.
Kotsko, Adam. *The Prince of This World*. Stanford, CA: Stanford University Press, 2016.
Kristeva, Julia. *Hatred and Forgiveness*. Translated by Jeanine Herman. New York: Columbia University Press, 2012.
Kristeva, Julia. *This Incredible Need to Believe*. Translated by Beverley Bie Brahic. New York: Columbia University Press, 2011.
Lacoste, Jean-Yves. *Experience and the Absolute: Disputed Questions on the Humanity of Man*. Translated by Mark Raftery-Skehan. New York: Fordham University Press, 2004.
Lacoste, Jean-Yves. *From Theology to Theological Thinking*. Translated by W. Chris Hackett. Charlottesville: University of Virginia Press, 2014.
Ladner, Gerhart B. *The Idea of Reform: Its Impact on Christian Thought and Action in the Age of the Fathers*. Cambridge, MA: Harvard University Press, 1959.
Latour, Bruno. *An Inquiry into Modes of Existence: An Anthropology of the Moderns*. Translated by Catherine Porter. Cambridge, MA: Harvard University Press, 2013.
Latour, Bruno. *On the Modern Cult of the Factish Gods*. Durham, NC: Duke University Press, 2010.
Levinas, Emmanuel. *Totality and Infinity: An Essay on Exteriority*. Translated by Alphonso Lingis. Pittsburgh, PA: Duquesne University, 1969.
Lyotard, Jean-François. *The Differend: Phrases in Dispute*. Translated by Georges Van Den Abbeele. Minneapolis: University of Minnesota Press, 1988.
Lyotard, Jean-François. *Lessons on the Analytic of the Sublime*. Translated by Elizabeth Rottenberg. Stanford: Stanford University Press, 1994.
Lyotard, Jean-François. *The Postmodern Condition: A Report on Knowledge*. Translated by Geoffrey Bennington and Brian Massumi. Minneapolis: University of Minnesota Press, 1984.
Manent, Pierre. *An Intellectual History of Liberalism*. Translated by Rebecca Balinski. Princeton, NJ: Princeton University Press, 1996.
Marcuse, Herbert. *The Aesthetic Dimension: Toward a Critique of Marxist Aesthetics*. Translated by Erica Sherover. Boston: Beacon, 1979.

Marion, Jean-Luc. *In Excess: Studies of Saturated Phenomena*. Translated by Robyn Horner and Vincent Berraud. New York: Fordham University Press, 2004.

Marion, Jean-Luc. *The Visible and the Revealed*. Translated by Christina Gschwandtner. New York: Fordham University Press, 2008.

Marion, Jean-Luc Marion. *Negative Certainties*. Translated by Stephen E. Lewis. Chicago: University of Chicago Press, 2015.

McBrien, Richard P. *The Church: The Evolution of Catholicism*. New York: HarperOne, 2008.

Menke, Christoph. *The Sovereignty of Art: Aesthetic Negativity in Adorno and Derrida*. Translated by Neil Solomon. Cambridge, MA: MIT Press, 1998.

Metz, Johann Baptist. *Faith in History and Society: Toward a Practical Fundamental Theology*. Translated by J. Matthew Ashley. New York: Crossroad, 2007.

Metz, Johann Baptist. *Poverty of Spirit*. Translated by John Drury. Mahwah, NJ: Paulist Press, 1968.

Milbank, John. *Beyond Secular Order: The Representation of Being and the Representation of the People*. Oxford: Wiley-Blackwell, 2013.

Milbank, John. "Materialism and Transcendence." In *Theology and the Political: The New Debate*. Edited by Creston Davis, John Milbank, and Slavoj Žižek. Durham, NC: Duke University Press, 2005.

Miller, Adam. *Speculative Grace: Bruno Latour and Object-Oriented Theology*. New York: Fordham University Press, 2013.

Moltmann, Jürgen. *The Crucified God: The Cross of Christ as the Foundation and Criticism of Christian Theology*. Translated by R. A. Wilson and John Bowden. Minneapolis, MN: Fortress, 1993.

Moltmann, Jürgen. *Theology of Hope: On the Ground and the Implications of a Christian Eschatology*. Translated by James W. Leitch. Minneapolis, MN: Fortress, 1967.

Moyn, Samuel. "Hannah Arendt on the Secular." *New German Critique* 35:3 (2008), pp. 71–96.

Nancy, Jean-Luc. *Dis-Enclosure: The Deconstruction of Christianity*. Translated by Bettina Bergo, Gabriel Malenfant, and Michael B. Smith. New York: Fordham University Press, 2008.

Nancy, Jean-Luc. "The Sublime Offering." In *A Finite Thinking*. Edited by Simon Sparks. Translated by Jeffrey Libbrett. Stanford: Stanford University Press, 2003.

Navone, John. *Triumph through Failure: A Theology of the Cross*. Homebush: St Paul, 1984.

Newheiser, David. *Hope in a Secular Age: Deconstruction, Negative Theology, and the Future of Faith*. Cambridge: Cambridge University Press, 2019.

Niebuhr, H. Richard. *Christ and Culture*. New York: Harper & Row, 1951.

Nietzsche, Friedrich. *Untimely Meditations*. Edited by Daniel Breazeale. Translated by R. J. Hollingdale. Cambridge: Cambridge University Press, 1997.

O'Murchu, Diarmuid. *Christianity's Dangerous Memory: A Rediscovery of the Revolutionary Jesus*. New York: Crossroad, 2011.

Orsi, Robert A. *History and Presence*. Cambridge, MA: Belknap Press, 2016.

Pillow, Kirk. *Sublime Understanding: Aesthetic Reflection in Kant and Hegel*. Cambridge, MA: MIT Press, 2000.

Pseudo-Dionysius. *The Complete Works*. Edited by Colm Luibhéid. Translated by Paul Rorem. Mahwah, NJ: Paulist Press, 1987.
Ricoeur, Paul. *Memory, History, Forgetting*. Translated by Kathleen Blamey and David Pellauer. Chicago: University of Chicago Press, 2006.
Ricoeur, Paul. "The Memory of Suffering." In *Figuring the Sacred: Religion, Narrative and Imagination*. Edited by Mark I. Wallace. Minneapolis, MN: Fortress Press, 1995.
Ricoeur, Paul. *On Translation*. Translated by Eileen Brennan. Abingdon: Routledge, 2006.
Ricoeur, Paul. *The Rule of Metaphor: The Creation of Meaning in Language*. Translated by Robert Czerny with Kathleen McLaughlin and John Costello. London: Routledge, 1978.
Ricoeur, Paul. *Time and Narrative*, vol. 3. Translated by Kathleen Blamey and David Pellauer. Chicago: University of Chicago Press, 1990.
Roberts, Louis. *The Theological Aesthetics of Hans Urs von Balthasar*. Washington, DC: Catholic University of America Press, 1987.
Roberts, Michelle Voss. *Dualities: A Theology of Difference*. Louisville, KY: Westminster John Knox Press, 2010.
Rose, Gillian. *The Melancholy Science: An Introduction to the Thought of Theodor W. Adorno*. London: Verso, 2014.
Rose, Marika. *A Theology of Failure: Žižek against Christian Innocence*. New York: Fordham University Press, 2019.
Rosen, Stanley. *Nihilism: A Philosophical Essay*. New Haven, CT: Yale University Press, 1969.
Ruether, Rosemary Radford. *The Church against Itself: An Inquiry into the Conditions of Historical Existence for the Eschatological Community*. New York: Herder & Herder, 1967.
Ruti, Mari. *The Singularity of Being: Lacan and the Immortal Within*. New York: Fordham University Press, 2012.
Sartre, Jean-Paul. *Critique of Dialectical Reason*, vol. 2. Translated by Quintin Hoare. London: Verso, 1991.
Schmitt, Carl. *The Concept of the Political*. Translated by George Schwab. Chicago: University of Chicago Press, 1996.
Schmitt, Carl. *Political Theology: Four Chapters on the Concept of Sovereignty*. Translated by George Schwab. Chicago: University of Chicago Press, 2005.
Schrijvers, Joeri. *Ontotheological Turnings? The Decentering of the Modern Subject in Recent French Phenomenology*. Albany, NY: SUNY Press, 2011.
Shapiro, Michael J. *The Political Sublime*. Durham, NC: Duke University Press, 2018.
Siedentop, Larry. *Inventing the Individual: The Origins of Western Liberalism*. Cambridge, MA: Belknap, 2014.
Slocombe, Will. *Nihilism and the Sublime Postmodern*. London: Routledge, 2005.
Sloterdijk, Peter. *Spheres: Vol. 1: Bubbles: Microspherology*. Translated by Wieland Hoban. South Pasadena, CA: Semiotext(e), 2011.
Taubes, Jacob. *The Political Theology of Saint Paul*. Translated by Dana Hollander. Stanford: Stanford University Press, 2003.

Taylor, Charles. "Preface." In *The Rivers North of the Future: The Testament of Ivan Illich as Told to David Cayley*. Edited by Ivan Illich and David Cayley. Toronto: Anansi, 2005.

Taylor, Charles. *A Secular Age*. Cambridge, MA: Belknap, 2007.

Taylor, Mark Lewis. *The Theological and the Political: On the Weight of the World*. Minneapolis, MN: Fortress, 2011.

Tracy, David. *The Analogical Imagination: Christ, Theology, and the Culture of Pluralism*. London: SCM Press, 1981.

Vardoulakis, Dimitris. *Sovereignty and Its Other: Toward the Dejustification of Violence*. New York: Fordham University Press, 2013.

Vattimo, Gianni. *Belief*. Translated by Luca D'Isanto and David Webb. Stanford: Stanford University Press, 1999.

Volf, Miroslav. *The End of Memory: Remembering Rightly in a Violent World*. Grand Rapids, MI: Eerdmans, 2006.

von Balthasar, Hans Urs. *The Glory of the Lord: A Theological Aesthetics, Volume V: The Realm of Metaphysics in the Modern Age*. San Francisco: Ignatius Press, 2011.

von Balthasar, Hans Urs. *The Theology of Karl Barth*. Translated by Edward T. Oakes. San Francisco: Ignatius Press, 1992.

Weber, Max. *The Protestant Ethic and the Spirit of Capitalism, and Other Writings*. Edited and translated by Peter Baehr and Gordon C. Wells. New York: Penguin, 2002.

Wolfson, Elliot R. *Open Secret: Postmessianic Messianism and the Mystical Revision of Menahem Mendel Schneerson*. New York: Columbia University Press, 2009.

Weller, Shane. *Modernism and Nihilism*. London: Palgrave and Macmillan, 2011.

Žižek, Slavoj. *Absolute Recoil: Towards a New Foundation of Dialectical Materialism*. London: Verso, 2014.

Žižek, Slavoj. *Less than Nothing: Hegel and the Shadow of Dialectical Materialism*. London: Verso, 2012.

Žižek, Slavoj. *The Sublime Object of Ideology*. London: Verso, 1989.

Žižek, Slavoj. *The Ticklish Subject: The Absent Centre of Political Ontology*. London: Verso, 2000.

Žižek, Slavoj. *Violence*. New York: Picador, 2008.

Žižek, Slavoj and John Milbank. *The Monstrosity of Christ: Paradox or Dialectic?* Edited by Creston Davis. Cambridge, MA: MIT Press, 2009.

INDEX

actuality 25, 28, 37, 59, 120–1
Adorno, Theodor 5–6, 11, 13, 20–2, 33–4, 39–50, 52, 64, 69, 72, 78, 83, 111, 133, 158, 161
Agamben, Giorgio 6–7, 18, 22, 25–6, 30–1, 33–4, 36–8, 42, 48, 58–62, 64, 66, 78, 80, 82, 90, 110, 112, 115–16, 121, 126, 132–3, 138–41, 143–8, 152, 160
alienation 34, 38, 56, 85
analogy 22, 28, 103, 105–10, 113, 118, 120–2
Ankersmit, Frank 101, 103, 114
antinomian 1, 16, 26, 30, 40, 43, 45, 50, 56–8, 60–2, 66, 68, 92, 101, 109–11, 136, 139, 146, 157–8
Andersen, Hans Christian 155
apophatic 14, 80, 158, 162 n.4
Aquinas, Thomas 107
Arendt, Hannah 7, 127–36, 138–41
Aristotle 120, 155
atheism 14, 19, 25, 34–8, 44, 51–2, 142, 159
Augustine 10, 152
Auschwitz 39–40, 42, 46, 119
autonomy 54, 78, 85, 145, 149, 154

Badiou, Alain 80
Barth, Karl 28, 87–8, 90
Bataille, Georges 94
Benjamin, Walter 7, 29–30, 42, 94, 103, 110, 115–16, 127, 131–40, 144, 146
Blondel, Maurice 6, 46, 49
Blumenberg, Hans 151–2
Boeve, Lieven 30
Bonhoeffer, Dietrich 40
Brassier, Ray 157
Bultmann, Rudolf 42, 44, 69, 111
Butler, Judith 34, 82, 176 n.3, 179 n.18

Calvin, John 87
Caputo, John 6, 10, 12–13, 15, 32, 34, 42, 44, 50, 65, 67–8, 77, 82, 92, 158–9
Chrétien, Jean-Louis 54

dangerous memory 103, 115, 125
death of God 1, 19, 25, 29, 35–6, 38, 48, 51–2, 81, 83, 95, 102, 113, 121, 142, 159, 161
de Certeau, Michel 62
de Vries, Hent 49–50
Derrida, Jacques 7, 10, 14–17, 19, 25, 30–1, 34, 37, 42, 44, 50, 65, 68, 80, 82, 110, 134–8, 140, 143
Descartes, Rene 117
différance 15, 17
disobedience 62–3, 126
division of division 32, 36–7, 48, 50, 143
Dorrien, Gary 90
Dostoyevsky, Fyodor 34
Dupuy, Jean-Pierre 142

Eagleton, Terry 83–91
Eckhart, Meister 10, 53
Esposito, Roberto 54, 156

Falque, Emmanuel 49
fetish 11, 37, 49, 59, 69–70, 72, 83, 153
Foucault, Michel 57, 61, 78, 131
Franciscan 26, 33, 95, 147–8, 163–4 n.28
Freud, Sigmund 31, 71
Friedlander, Eli 6, 71, 77
Fromm, Erich 62–3

Gadamer, Hans-Georg 79, 105
Gauchet, Marcel 33
Girard, René 7, 20–2, 24, 35, 47, 99, 100–3, 105–6, 110–12, 114, 122, 133, 142–3
Goux, Jean-Joseph 182 n.7

Halík, Tomáš 5, 10–13, 15, 17, 35–6
Haynes, Patrice 42, 44
Hegel, G.W.F. 6, 27–31, 33, 36, 131, 133, 143, 158
Heidegger, Martin 26, 33, 39, 113, 120
Hemming, Laurence Paul 114, 121–2
heresy 1–2, 30, 37–8, 42–3, 57, 61, 109, 157–8
Horkheimer, Max 47
Husserl, Edmund 11
hypernomian 15, 30, 37, 45, 57, 61, 66, 74, 93, 116

ideology 10, 12, 14, 26–7, 44, 48, 50, 59, 63, 68, 70, 83–5, 98–101, 105–6, 119, 128, 157
Illich, Ivan 6, 55–8, 60–2, 66, 70, 96
immanence 2, 6–7, 39–41, 45–7, 49, 51–2, 64, 69, 81, 90, 118, 120, 122, 136, 140, 143, 153, 159

Jefferson, Thomas 138
John of the Cross 10
Joyce, James 52

Kant, Immanuel 6, 35, 67–9, 71–7, 84–5, 87–93, 98, 114, 116–18, 120, 122, 126
Kantorowicz, Ernst 156
kataphatic 14, 158
Kearney, Richard 117
Keats, John 172 n.12
Keller, Catherine 155
kenosis 4, 16, 51, 53, 78, 92, 94, 160, 161
Kierkegaard, Søren 10–13, 20–2, 24, 27–9, 31, 35, 88, 140, 153–4
Kingdom of God 65, 80–1, 123, 125, 143
Kristeva, Julia 6, 52–3

Lacoste, Jean-Yves 116
Ladner, Gerhart 62–4
Latour, Bruno 162 n.3
Levinas, Emmanuel 44, 68, 134
Luther, Martin 41, 131
Lyotard, Jean-François 74, 107, 118–19, 160

Machiavelli, Niccolò 152
Marion, Jean-Luc 10–11, 24, 49, 114, 116–17
Marx, Karl 62, 143–4, 153
materialism 13, 41–3, 50, 62–4, 70, 112, 114, 117, 136–7, 141, 143, 147, 153
messianic 15, 32, 45, 48, 50, 56, 58, 61–2, 112, 132, 158, 160
  hope 136
  promise 161
  suspension 127, 138–9, 144, 146–7
  time 116
  as weak force 29–30, 37, 42–3, 50, 80, 82, 103, 110, 138–9, 146, 160
metaphor 14, 103, 106–8, 118–22
Melville, Herman 25
Menke, Christoph 78
Metz, Johann Baptist 30, 46, 49, 92–5, 103
Milbank, John 13, 28, 35, 60–1, 107
minimal theology 49–51, 53, 64, 66, 73, 75, 78, 96–7, 122, 147, 157, 159
Moltmann, Jürgen 38, 41, 48–50
mystical 5, 10, 92, 111, 134, 158, 159

Nancy, Jean-Luc 32–3, 159
negation of negation 13–14, 19, 27–32, 34–6, 38, 41–2, 47, 50, 66, 91, 93, 143, 149
negative 5, 11, 14–15, 17, 22, 25–6, 41, 45, 53, 69, 71, 74, 94, 101, 143
  dialectic 5, 13, 20–2, 28, 35–7, 40, 42–6, 48, 68, 78, 91, 107–8, 113
  eschatology 13, 17, 83
  theology 5, 10, 13–17, 19, 27, 30, 34, 39, 89, 136, 158
Newman, John Henry 72, 84
Niebuhr, H. Richard 126
Nietzsche, Friedrich 77, 88, 90, 105–7, 109
nihilism 45, 52, 67–8, 80, 92, 94, 136–7, 157–8

obedience 62, 83, 126, 128, 161
orthodoxy 1–3, 5, 13, 28, 35, 37–8, 55, 57–9, 66, 71, 73, 78–9, 86, 90, 109, 129, 144, 148, 157

Paul, Saint 5, 10, 17–19, 21, 31–3, 36–7, 48, 60, 63, 65–6, 80–2, 91, 93–5, 110, 142–4, 146–7, 161
Pillow, Kirk 79
Plato 148
potentiality 25–6, 28, 92, 120–1, 146, 157
precariousness 7, 31, 99, 104, 115–16
profanation 25, 38, 59, 66, 115, 139–41, 144, 146
Pseudo-Dionysius 11

Rahner, Karl 12
Reformation 65, 86, 131, 152
resurrection 9, 41, 43–5, 48, 103
revolution 5, 7, 29, 22, 86, 125–6, 128–34, 138–41, 143–6, 148, 151, 157
Ricoeur, Paul 19, 54, 80, 102–10, 116, 120–2
Rose, Marika 161
Rosen, Stanley 68
Ruether, Rosemary Radford 46

Sartre, Jean-Paul 134, 137, 159
Schmitt, Carl 12, 18, 23–5, 28–9, 78, 85, 102, 126–7, 140, 153–4
Schopenhauer, Arthur 77, 88
Siedentop, Larry 161

Sloterdijk, Peter 159–61
sovereignty 2–3, 12–13, 23–9, 34, 37, 39–40, 48, 51, 54–5, 59, 75, 78, 83–4, 86–7, 90–1, 102, 104, 111, 119, 123, 127, 131–2, 134–5, 137, 140, 142, 149, 153–7, 159
Spinoza, Baruch 39, 153

Taubes, Jacob 80
Taylor, Charles 6, 53–9, 61, 66, 79, 87–91, 96, 125
Taylor, Mark Lewis 1
Tracy, David 105, 107, 109
transcendence 2, 6, 14, 16, 39–41, 45–6, 51–2, 59, 64, 66, 69, 76, 89, 95, 114, 120–2, 136, 153, 159–61

Vardoulakis, Dimitris 142
Vattimo, Gianni 111
Volf, Miroslav 109
von Balthasar, Hans Urs 28, 88–91, 107

Weber, Max 152
Wolfson, Elliot 15, 37, 93

Žižek, Slavoj 7, 13, 16, 26, 28, 30, 32–6, 38, 44, 53, 60, 68, 80, 106, 140–5, 158